the Perfect BrainWash

More playtime, less anxiety with AdEd Tech

Hannes De Wachter

© Copyright 2022 - All rights reserved.

The content contained within this book may not be reproduced, duplicated or transmitted without direct written permission from the author or the publisher.

Under no circumstances will any blame or legal responsibility be held against the publisher, or author, for any damages, reparation, or monetary loss due to the information contained within this book. Either directly or indirectly.

Legal Notice:

This book is copyright protected. This book is only for personal use. You cannot amend, distribute, sell, use, quote or paraphrase any part, or the content within this book, without the consent of the author or publisher.

Disclaimer Notice:

Please note the information contained within this document is for educational and entertainment purposes only. All effort has been executed to present accurate, up to date, and reliable, complete information. No warranties of any kind are declared or implied. Readers acknowledge that the author is not engaging in the rendering of legal, financial, medical or professional advice. The content within this book has been derived from various sources. Please consult a licensed professional before attempting any techniques outlined in this book.

By reading this document, the reader agrees that under no circumstances is the author responsible for any losses, direct or indirect, which are incurred as a result of the use of the information contained within this document, including, but not limited to, — errors, omissions, or inaccuracies.

Contents

Preface: Mindlessness   11
Introduction - The who and the why   15

1. Regulating AdTech sooner or later?   23
2. Doing the groundwork: philosophical and scientific underpinnings to solving big problems   43
3. Trends in (consumer) neuroscience   73
4. Advanced techniques in consumer neuroscience   97
5. The "freemium" kiss of death   117
6. Making capitalism work for us: How research bridges the gap between advertising and education   143
7. Democratizing Consumer Neuroscience   159
8. Corporate soul mates and Brand Equity   173
9. the ultimate teasers - Education on autopilot   189
10. Homo Ludens and 'AdEdTech'   207

Recommended reading   223
Notes   229

"Our age is seeking a new spring of life. I found one and drank of it and the water tasted good."

— C.G. Jung

Thank you

This book is made possible thanks to a number of extraordinary people who are close to my heart.

I want to thank my highschool sweetheart, Lobke, who continues to 'stand by me' ever since we danced to the tune on our beautiful April 2006 wedding day. It's amazing how we still complement each other to find balance and synergies in our fortunate lives. Thanks, honey, from the bottom of my heart for putting up with my restless mind.

Thanks also to my wonderful children, Arthur and Olivia, who inspired me to write this book and allow me to experience unconditional love. I encourage them to stay humble, be 'response-able', and explore life.

I thank my loving parents, who've demonstrated the power of leading by example, my caring sisters and supportive in-laws. Being part of such a tight knit family has no doubt turned me into the person that I am today, grateful and optimistic, but also adventurous, ambitious and poised to give back.

Finally, this book would never have happened were it not for my publisher and executive producer. Thanks, Aisha for reaching out and convincing me to take a chance. And respect to you, Natalie for helping me crystallize my monkey brain ideas and put pen to paper.

All those close to me over the last decade have contributed indirectly to the ideas behind this book (sorry about that) and I consider you all part of a community that I hope, by spreading the word, will ignite a fire into the minds of many of your own community members.

Preface: Mindlessness

We prefer the familiar. The things we recognise because they consistently appear to us in the same context. The things that frequently "co-occur" as AI scientists would describe it. Understanding co-occurrence patterns brings the promise of ever more accurate predictions. Through science, we seek to decode and predict nature because it offers us peace of mind, material comfort, and a sense of life control. Through neuroscience (humanity's quest to understand the biological basis of learning, memory, perception, and consciousness), we are starting to predict human behavior with startling accuracy.

Familiarity is the reason why we are willing to pay more for a 'real' Coca-Cola than an unfamiliar brand (that might even taste better according to blindfolded testing). This is why Coca-Cola, Apple, and Lego are some of the most preferred brands worldwide. Brands that carry the highest "brand equity". They've been delivering on their brand promise even before you gained self awareness. They became the hallmark brands of western pop culture, which many entrepreneurs and influencers look up to as role models. You've learned to love them below conscious awareness. They've created familiarity on auto-pilot, with their advertisers schooling you with countless branding campaigns.

Familiarizing you with brands is the bread and butter of the advertising sector that makes up the fuel that fires our economic engines. It's the world of advertising that's financing many of your life experiences directly or indirectly through social media and free user experiences.

But there's a caveat that comes with this model. One that's causing an alarming increase in mental disease. A form of attrition that's slowly but steadily deteriorating our cultural and ethical standards.

Too many of our children don't particularly like school. They associate school with (home)work. Their dislike implies they are less likely to feel motivated to learn the educational content they are being provided. Lack of motivation translates into suboptimal grades. Poor grades are indicative of less educated children, more susceptible to fake news, polarizing conspiracy theories, and general anxiety.

Children spend much of their time consuming content 'recommended' to them online. Much of this content is directly or indirectly sponsored by managers incentivized to encourage consumption. Moreover, this content is being 'recommended' to our children in their social media 'feeds' by algorithms programmed to promote the brands that bid the most for our online attention.

If the world's most popular platforms and leading AI algorithms are designed to encourage advertisers to buy and *talk* rather than *walk* their talk, should we be surprised that mental illness is skyrocketing? Should we trust our kids to get schooled by influencers looking to score a lucrative brand endorsement?

This book offers surprisingly simple yet bold ideas to improve mental health through the synergetic effect of merging Advertising Technology (AdTech) with Education Technology (EdTech). We're not as helpless as you might think. The courage to speak up and voice your concerns is the catalyst for change. Even as you read this book, you're already helping to turn the tide by increasing your understanding of the problem. You will then discover how simple and practical a solution can be. One that's been hiding in plain sight.

Introduction - The who and the why

The intuitive mind is a sacred gift and the rational mind is a faithful servant. We have created a society that honors the servant and has forgotten the gift.

- Albert Einstein[1]

Welcome to The Perfect Brain*Wash*.

Over the course of this book, we're going to look at the ways in which our current media landscape, and advertising in particular, is programming our children. It's changing how they interact with the world around them and, more importantly, it's changing how they interact with each other.

This isn't even close to being a new topic. Concerns are raised at the advent of every new technology, and the refrain "think of the children" has been overused to the point of farce. Why, then, do you need to read this book?

You need to read this book because, as an economist, having worked nearly a decade with academic researchers, I've seen that the warnings are substantially more justified this time and profoundly more urgent.

More importantly, I'm not here to spread doom and gloom. I want to offer solutions.

After starting my career in finance and technology transfer, I've spent the last decade taking a deep dive into the advertising technology ("AdTech") sector, focusing on behavioral economics and consumer neuroscience. Despite the prejudice many people seem to have against the advertising sector (and those who choose to work as marketers), I've always tried to retain a scientific mindset and ethical framework to navigate my own path and increase my understanding of this captivating sector.

Since moving into the marketing and advertising technology sector, I have been trying to find ways for science and technology to reconcile business with social needs. Over the past decade, I've tried to reduce my blind spots and sought to democratize consumer neuroscience by building a semantic research platform.

One of the privileges of having worked as a university technology transfer manager is that I have been able to form contacts and connections with entrepreneurial scientists, researchers, and thinkers from a wide variety of disciplines.

No man is an island - John Donne

The same is true of ideas. While I take full responsibility for the ideas I'm presenting in this book, I certainly can't take all of the credit. They are the product of countless conversations with people working in disciplines as diverse as neuroscience, philosophy, and artificial intelligence. This book is my attempt to connect the dots.

Despite the scale of the problem, it has become clear that no single field has the answer.

Importantly, neither science nor technology can actually solve this problem. They will likely be an essential component of any solution, but they can't *be* the solution or *create* the solution.

The only person who can do that is you... or, more precisely, all of us: you, your family, your friends, your children, trainers, colleagues, team members, community leaders, neighbors, teachers, politicians, and so on., ... Every member of your community is within your sphere of influence.

Many of the changes I want to make are going to require significant political action. There will need to be legislation and regulation, but it will need to be the right kind of regulation and legislation. Knee-jerk reactions or public panic could do more harm than good.

Political action will only happen if there's sufficient pressure, and, for that, we need a population that both understands the problem and requires that it be fixed properly. This is where you come in.

One of my biggest motivations in writing this book was to offer real, achievable solutions to what I see as one of the biggest threats to our future. In all honesty, I'm an optimist. I don't want to just repeat the message that "our children are being brainwashed through advertising." I want to contribute what I can to solving the problem.

We do need to look at what the problem is, understand it, and gain an accurate sense of the scale of the task ahead of us. But we then have to act.

I don't want to leave you feeling hopeless. Instead, I want to empower you with a range of 'therapies' to treat the problem. I'll say several times throughout this book that advertisers aren't the enemy, but they are a huge part of the solution.

When I talk about "treatments" and "therapies" for the mental attrition we are witnessing, I want you to know that we're going to be going somewhere new and innovative. This isn't about sticking on a band-aid. These treatments are going to address the real root of the problem, and that's important.

All too often, parents who express their concerns about the impact of advertising on their children are bombarded with well-meaning advice. Much of this comes from older relatives who believe that telling a 10-year old that they're too young to have a phone is a "straightforward, common-sense solution!"

There are two problems with this type of solution. Firstly, they simply don't reflect the world we actually live in. Our solutions need to be innovative and far-reaching, but we also need to be able to see the achievable steps that can bring us there.

The second problem is that these remedies only protect your children, and usually only while they're under your direct supervision. We all want our children to become capable, independent young adults, but we also want them to be safe. Keeping our children safe from social ills by changing *them* will only ever be a partial success. Wouldn't it be better to change *society* to fit their needs?

An inadequate 'therapy' could prove even more problematic than our current situation. Even worse, a failed attempt at regulating and reforming the advertising and marketing industries could reinforce the impression that certain companies are just too large to control, and that we simply have to ameliorate their actions as best we can.

To this end, the solutions I offer towards the end of this book have drawn from the very latest theories and strategies. The areas I've drawn on most heavily have been philosophy of mind, cognitive psychology, and behavioral economics. These are not my only sources of inspiration, but they have had the greatest influence on the suggestions I've offered.

I'm really grateful that you're joining me on this journey. This is a change that we can only make together. For my part, I'm going to show you the most up-to-date thinking and cutting-edge science that has shaped my thoughts. We'll then take a deep look at several possible solutions, exploring how they might work and what risks, if any, will need to be addressed.

For your part, I only ask that you keep an open mind and enjoy the journey.

Chapter 1
Regulating AdTech sooner or later?

"AI doesn't have to be evil to destroy humanity – if AI has a goal and humanity just happens to come in the way, it will destroy humanity as a matter of course without even thinking about it, no hard feelings."

- Elon Musk

Chapter 1 Executive Summary:

- The frequency and sophistication of advertising has increased significantly over the last decades.
- Children's education is happening online, increasingly intertwined with advertising in disguise.

- The WHO is reporting an exponential rise in depression, anxiety, and other forms of mental illness in children, even at very young ages.
- We are facing a pivotal moment in time for calling upon advertisers to shift to a human-centric artificial intelligence when it comes to the adoption of neuromarketing.

Understanding the scale of the problem

If we're going to talk about the "problem" of advertising, especially that aimed at our children, the first thing we need to understand is just how much advertising we are actually exposed to. It often doesn't *feel* as though we're being bombarded with constant exhortations to buy a particular product or pay for a specific service.

Estimates of how many ads the average person sees per day vary wildly. In fairness to the researchers, so does internet use and accessibility to advertisers. An elderly person without a smartphone probably sees far fewer daily ads than your average teenager, for example.

Still, even the lower-end estimates of how many advertisements we see per day can seem shocking. In 2017, it was estimated that we saw between 4,000 and 10,000 ads per person per day. The figure today is almost certainly significantly higher.

So why don't we feel bombarded? Some of us do. Many people feel that advertising has gotten out of control, though this is skewed towards older people. Which gives us our first clue.

We've come to see this level of advertising as "normal". We tune it out. We barely notice the adverts themselves. We leave adverts as soon as we can, and become frustrated at unskippable adverts during streaming services. We've become the proverbial "boiled frog".

It's also worth realizing that a lot of the marketing content that we see doesn't register as such. In the days before the internet, adverts were clearly identifiable. They were what happened on TV in between sections of the TV show we were watching. Now, however, they have become far more subtle.

Many social media influencers and content providers produce paid content that merges seamlessly into their normal content. It can be challenging to draw the line between communicating personal preferences and advertising.

If I don't notice it, does it matter?

When asked about the amount of advertising they see on a daily basis, the majority of people don't accept that it's so substantial. Once they realize it's true, however, their response changes. They ask a perfectly reasonable question.

"If I'm not even noticing the adverts, do they matter?"

Unfortunately, the answer from cognitive neuroscience is completely clear. Yes. It absolutely matters.

Your brain is always working, and it processes far more data about the world than you are aware of. For decades now, psychologists and neuroscientists have been using a tool known as the "forced-choice task". In a forced-choice paradigm experiment, you are presented with several stimuli, such as words or pictures, in such a way that you don't realize you've seen them. Typically, they are presented too quickly for you to take them in. If you are asked what you saw, you don't have an answer. If you are asked to choose between two different options, however, you'll pick the right one.

This technique has been used time after time to investigate all kinds of aspects of our thinking, and we know it works. We have concrete evidence that things we don't notice are still being processed by our brains.

In some ways, the ads you don't notice might be more worrying, as they bypass your rational mind.

When it comes to your children, the situation is even more stark.

The impact of advertising on children

When we talk about the impact of advertising on children, we're typically not talking about them making poor purchasing decisions or getting themselves into debt (although this is not entirely unheard of). Our bigger concern is the impact it has on their developing brains.

For the purposes of this explanation, we're going to think of the brain as a collection of connections. Many of us are used to talking about 'brain cells', but it's actually the connections (technically, these are called synapses) between these cells that matter.

Each brain cell can have hundreds, thousands, or even tens of thousands of connections, and will often have a large number of different connections to the same cell.

We intuitively assume that children are born with minimal connections and that they build new connections as they learn. Unfortunately, biology isn't always logical.

In fact, children are born with far more connections than they need. Their stages of development are largely linked to periods of "synaptic pruning", where excess connections are allowed to die off. This synaptic pruning keeps the connections that have been the most active and allows inactive connections to lapse. This makes the brain more efficient, which allows the development we see in their behavior.

But what happens when adverts come into the mix? Adverts are (mostly) visual stimuli designed to attract our attention and change our emotions and behavior in specific ways. Children have no defenses against those intentions. By spending their formative years being presented with advertisements, practicing ignoring them intellectually, whilst not creating defenses against their influence, children are being made more malleable.

Great for advertisers. Not necessarily so great for humanity.

I don't know of anyone who is comfortable with their children being manipulated below conscious awareness.

How did we get into this situation?

It's important to emphasize that I'm not suggesting that advertisers are deliberately *aiming* to make our children more malleable. I'm merely pointing out that they *are*. This is an almost inevitable consequence of placing a developing brain in an environment with near-constant access to advertising content.

We need to recognize that companies and organizations aren't actually malevolent entities that exist outside of society. Companies are our creations. Even some of the great behemoths of our time were founded by an individual or a small team, and often not particularly long ago.

Companies are founded by people who live in the same society that we do. Those founders find great employees, who also live within our social structures. Those employees work hard and try to create products and services that people will value.

No one is setting out to harm our children, or society at large. But business can sometimes be a cutthroat place. Small start-ups are often ambitious, socially-conscious communities, but the businesses are often extremely vulnerable. Larger companies may seem better able to survive the transition to a more socially-responsible advertising model, but their every move is watched and can have enormous consequences for their share price.

The neuromarketing techniques we're going to look at in this book are extremely effective, and therein lies our concern. Businesses often can't afford to pass up technologies and tactics that are being employed by their competitors.

This observation leads to an inevitable conclusion. Changing our advertising ecosystem for the better depends on our ability to make those changes profitable, or at least to ensure that they don't reduce a company's competitiveness.

We're not powerless

All this can leave us with feelings of profound powerlessness. Advertising is everywhere, and we know it's harming our children. The more we investigate the scale of the problem, the harder it can be to see a path out of the predicament we're in.

The balance of power feels deeply skewed, and not in our favor. We can't escape the endless advertising efforts ourselves. How can we possibly help our children to manage it? After a while, the problem seems too large for us to fix, and maybe even so large that it can't be fixed.

These feelings of powerlessness are understandable, but they're also probably the biggest obstacle to our being able to create meaningful change. When a problem seems beyond our ability to influence, our minds protect us by avoiding thinking about it. We define it as "just one of those things" or "the price of living in the modern world".

This is also probably the biggest motivator for me to write this book. We might feel tiny and powerless in the face of huge corporations, and their even larger advertising budgets, but this is an illusion. We're their customers, their service users, and their client base. We're also employees, voters, and activists.

The kind of change we need to protect our children is nothing less than radical social change, but we *are* society. Individually, we might feel powerless. As a community, we are empowered.

If we want to create change, we're going to have to change how we think about the world

If the words "radical social change" rang alarm bells for you, I understand. The form of capitalism we live under, and the scale and power of corporations, seem to have followed an inexorable path towards where we are today. The idea of making a significant change, or even worse, "radical change", can seem like a far higher risk than we're willing to pay.

But what if I were to tell you that the most radical change we're going to make is going to happen inside your own mind? Yes, there are aspects of our current social and economic system that will need to change, but the most radical thing that we can do is to change how we see the world around us.

Creating the kind of change that we're looking for means we're going to need to come up with innovative solutions. Before we can make changes that will protect our children, we need to believe that there really is a possible future where we succeed. We need to be able to imagine a world where corporations and advertisers are induced to use their enormous powers for the good of society as a whole, without damaging our social, political, and economic systems.

If that idea seems radical, that's OK. If it's hard to imagine just yet, that's OK too. Over the course of this book, we're going to explore how we can interact with the world in a different way, and ensure that powerful corporations and entities start to do their share as well.

Why is now the right time?

So why is this becoming such a big issue now?

The issue of marketing aimed at children has been concerning parents, teachers, and pediatricians for some time now. Recently, however, a number of factors have been converging, which means that the situation is becoming urgent.

The amount of advertising we are exposed to is increasing exponentially. Previously, children would only have been targeted for marketing purposes during television programming aimed directly at them. This was a maximum of just a few hours per day. They would also not have been exposed to advertising aimed at adults.

As the internet has become increasingly integrated into our lives, it has become more and more difficult to minimize children's exposure to all forms of advertising. In particular, the COVID-19 pandemic and increasing geopolitical tensions have led to a significant portion of even very young children's education taking place online. This has accelerated an already-rapid increase in the amount of advertising our children are exposed to.

At the same time, the strategies used by advertisers and marketers have also become increasingly sophisticated, which unfortunately means that they present more danger to children's development than ever before.

As parents, it is also becoming increasingly difficult to monitor children's internet use adequately. Children are being supplied with phones at ever younger ages. This is often designed to help keep them safe, but it makes it difficult to monitor their usage directly.

We're forced to rely on tech solutions to keep them safe online. Typically, these are designed to protect them from explicit material, gambling, and extremist content. We don't yet have adequate solutions to help minimize their exposure to marketing.

Without wanting to seem alarmist, we might be reaching the threshold of the last opportunity to check the ethical reach of the new age of advertisers. I've already mentioned that the impact on children's brains is making them more malleable. We like to think of our children as tech-savvy and socially aware, but their brains might be another matter.

As adults who have witnessed the dramatic increase in advertising during our lifetimes, we understand that this kind of bombardment is neither inevitable nor normal. Our lives weren't nearly as technological as our children's, and the advertising we were exposed to was easier for our brains to handle.

The effects of this bombardment can be seen in the exponential rise of depression, anxiety, and other forms of mental illness in children, even at very young ages. Globally, one in seven 10-19-year-olds experiences a mental disorder, accounting for 13% of the global burden of disease in this age group, according to November 2021 figures published by the World Health Organization (WHO). Depression, anxiety, and behavioral disorders are among the leading causes of illness and disability among adolescents. Suicide is the fourth leading cause of death among 15-19-year-olds. The consequences of failing to address adolescent mental health conditions extend to adulthood, impairing both physical and mental health and limiting opportunities to lead fulfilling lives as adults. These alarming figures coincide with observations of increasingly materialistic worldviews among the young, often fuelled by constant comparisons with international peers, which have been magnified by social media. According to the WHO, media influence and gender norms exacerbate the disparity between an adolescent's lived reality and their perceptions or aspirations for the future. Adolescents with mental health conditions are particularly vulnerable to social exclusion, discrimination, stigma (affecting readiness to seek help), educational difficulties, risk-taking behaviours, physical ill-health, and human rights violations. None of these are things that we want for our children.

We are in a position to see the scale of the AdTech bombardment fallout, as well as the advantages that those same technologies have brought us. Our children won't have that luxury. If we don't take action now, they may be left to fight a rearguard action for generations to come.

Neuromarketing: the future of advertising and marketing technology?

One of the biggest innovations in marketing, and the one that is leading to our particular concern, is neuromarketing. We're going to look at some of the different tools and techniques of neuromarketing throughout this book, but let's get a brief overview first.

Neuromarketing refers to the use of sophisticated techniques originally developed to understand how the brain processes different stimuli to guide product and marketing decisions.

From that description, neuromarketing might not sound too scary. After all, it's just using a different set of data to help them make marketing decisions. They might have made the same decisions anyway, right?

Unfortunately, neuromarketing isn't always as benign as it sounds. When researchers (and, by extension, companies) are able to "see" into our brains, they're able to predict our decisions and actions with far higher accuracy than we are able to do ourselves.

Now it sounds a little scarier, right?

Honestly, the appropriate level of concern at the moment is somewhere between those two levels. Yes, these tools offer insights that are substantially more meaningful than what researchers could gain through focus groups and traditional market research. But they're not at the level of being able to use the data they've gathered to manipulate our decisions on an individual level yet (although the popular Netflix documentary "The Social Dilemma" already suggests otherwise).

Where this technology might go in the future if left unchecked is, sadly, beyond the scope of this book. With dedication, and more than a little luck, we may still be able to check these developments before they become unmanageable.

Neuromarketing is uniquely worrisome for children

Neuromarketing is typically aimed at adults. After all, it's difficult to imagine many parents willing to offer their young children for brain scans to help with market research. I imagine that most PR and legal departments would also point out the obvious (and probably inevitable) PR disaster that would arise if they started carrying out this kind of research.

This doesn't mean that we don't need to worry, however. Although children aren't targeted by neuromarketing directly, they are still directly impacted by it. The tools that work so well for adults are turbo-charged when they're applied to our children.

We are going to talk later about the ways in which children are more vulnerable to advertising, especially techniques that focus on creating an emotional response. Any parent knows that advertisements can create an emotional "need" in a child for the latest product. We tend to assume that these must-have toys are "just a fad," and we don't really think about what our children are learning from their experiences with advertising.

The child who has the latest item becomes suddenly popular. Although our brains are highly developed, there are still many areas of the world where we are still responding with our 'monkey brain'. Our desire for social status is one such 'monkey brain' moment.

To the monkey brain, and young children, being popular is actually a matter of survival. They are fully dependent on the protection of others. At this level, being ostracized isn't just unpleasant. It's a question of life or death, or so their brain is telling them.

When young children, in particular, are presented with this kind of advertising, they start to internalize the suggestion that we can purchase our way to safety and security, along with many other messages. These unconscious beliefs are carried with us long into adulthood, and many are never adequately addressed or overcome.

No hand-wringing, please. We're finding solutions

As I've already mentioned, there are solutions to this problem. Our current situation is not inevitable. It is urgent, however.

These major companies are not going to make the changes we need out of sheer altruism. Our aim will be twofold. Firstly, we need to create social change that produces smarter, more equitable business models that help level the playing field for ethical underdog brands. Simply put, we need to make doing the right thing for our children also mean doing the right thing for their balance sheets. Secondly, we need to generate significant political pressure in favor of very specific regulations.

Saying "we need to regulate" isn't specific enough. The advertising sector has already adopted proprietary ethical charters to fend off more stringent regulation. The problem is these charters are slow to reflect both the threats and opportunities resulting from technological paradigm shifts in the fields of artificial intelligence and neuroscience, for example. We need to have clear guiding principles and ethical boundaries, backed by theory and evidence. We need the advertising sector to operate in a legal framework that reflects and protects human values.

More than anything, we need to present people with clear answers. Because these are difficult questions, and time is running out.

Chapter 2
Doing the groundwork: philosophical and scientific underpinnings to solving big problems

"Everything we call real is made of things that cannot be regarded as real. If quantum mechanics hasn't profoundly shocked you, you haven't understood it yet."

— Niels Bohr

Chapter 2 Executive Summary:

- An increasing body of academic research in the field of Psychology, Physics, Biology and Philosophy is pointing towards a more idealistic (subjective) worldview as opposed to a materialistic (objective) one, supported by advertising.
- The neuroscience of higher cognitive processes

(consciousness) is only just beginning. A field capturing an increasing amount of interest from the advertising sector.
- Philosophical metaphors help catalyze the paradigm shift required to innovate the advertising sector.
- Old publications by controversial scientists, such as Carl. G. Jung and Rupert Sheldrake, supporting the paradigm shift are being revisited in the context of new neuroscientific insights.

If we're going to properly understand (and address) the challenges raised in the previous chapter, it's going to be important to understand the problem in context. Although I'm primarily interested in finding solutions, these need to fit within how we understand the world. This means we need to examine some of the most radical and innovative thinking currently taking place in philosophy, physics, psychology, neuroscience, and biology.

In this chapter, we're going to take a (necessarily brief) tour around some of the cutting-edge thoughts, principles, and priorities across academia and see how they relate to our central premise.

The philosophy of consciousness

Philosophy might seem quite a distance away from being relevant to how we protect our children from the negative effects of excessive targeted advertisements on their minds. However, philosophers have been advancing their insights and metaphors to help us understand the human condition and find meaning in life since Plato illustrated the virtual nature of our reality with his cave metaphor—Plato illustrated how lifelong chained prisoners looking only at shadows of their guards on a cave wall mistake and inflate the two-dimensional shadows for their three-dimensional sources. Fast forwarding Plato's metaphor to this day, we see some of our children inflating their own virtual realities.

If we want to understand the human mind, we need to start by having a brief theory of consciousness. Consciousness is something that we all take for granted. You're familiar with Descartes' popular idea that "I think, therefore I am," but current thinking around the state of human consciousness is significantly more nuanced. Even the founding fathers of physicalist science, Descartes and Newton themselves, already knew that "a purely materialistic pattern of nature is utterly impossible". The 'hard problem' back in those seventeenth century days (referred to by Gilbert Ryle as the 'ghost in the machine') was not solved; "rather it was abandoned, as, over time, science turned to its more post-Newtonian course," as Noam Chomsky reminds us. "It was the machine that Newton exorcized, leaving the ghost intact. The 'hard problem' of the materialists disappeared, and there has been little noticeable progress in addressing other 'hard problems' that seemed no less mysterious to Descartes, Newton, Locke, and other leading figures.

In the summary of his life's work and reflections, "What Kind of Creatures are we?", Chomsky goes on:

> *"It has become standard practice in recent years to describe the problem of consciousness as 'the hard problem,' others being within our grasp, now or down the road. I think there are reasons for some skepticism, particularly when we recognize how sharply understanding declines beyond the simplest systems of nature. To illustrate with a few examples, a review article by Eric Kandel and Larry Squire on the current state of efforts aimed at 'breaking down scientific barriers to the study of brain and mind' concludes that 'the*

neuroscience of higher cognitive processes is only beginning'."

Indeed, the quest to understand human consciousness has recently been gaining momentum, and not only in academic circles. Understanding consciousness brings the promise of helping us understand ourselves, how we influence each other, and how we're influenced in turn. This can both inform our understanding of how our children are being influenced by the media environment they are exposed to and how we can influence others to achieve our goals.

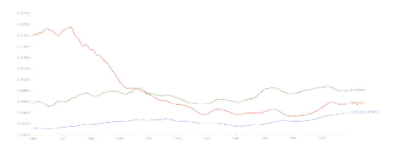

Figure 1 (Google Books Ngram Viewer)

When you enter the words 'consciousness', 'religion' and 'science' into the Google Books Ngram Viewer, it displays a graph illustrating how often those words have occurred in a corpus of books over the selected years. Whereas for the word 'religion' the trend since the year

1800 has clearly been downward, the appearance of the word 'consciousness' in popular literature has more than doubled and appears to be catching up to 'religion' in terms of popularity.

Source: https://books.google.com/ngrams

Kastrup's whirlpool metaphor

One of the most influential (and innovative) thinkers currently working in the philosophy of mind is Bernardo Kastrup. As you might expect, his ideas are deeply nuanced and can be difficult to follow, but we're just going to take a few moments to cover the basics.

Within the philosophy of mind, there are two schools of thought; materialism and idealism. Materialism is the belief in the primacy of the physical world around us, *made up of* ever smaller 'elementary' particles like atoms, protons, quarks, leptons, and the Higgs boson 'God' particle, the so-called building blocks of physical matter. Idealism is the belief that consciousness is the primordial substrate that transcends the 'Big Bang' particle theory and should be the primary way in which we understand the world around us. Under idealism, matter is nothing but a conscious sensory experience that *feels* tangible but is virtual and subjective in essence. In this view, matter could be considered similar to the computer generated stimuli experienced in a full immersive, haptic feedback virtual reality game. For idealists, physics represents a practical, *quantitative* expression, a ruleset used to communicate, and predict our *qualitative* nature. In other words, for idealists, physics represents the programming language of our virtual reality.

This might sound a little confusing, but there are some important ideas behind this. In a materialistic worldview, everything we experience comes to us through the medium of our senses. Our brain responds to outside 'physical' stimuli, such as light photons hitting our eyes or sound waves making parts of our ears vibrate, which then leads to our experience of those stimuli.

In an idealistic approach, that same brain response momentarily captured (e.g. through a brain scan) is simply the outward manifestation of a conscious, essentially qualitative experience. The snapshot is used to communicate the qualitative states many of us seem to share. So far, such brain scans have generally been used to diagnose mental disease due to high imaging costs. But as these costs continue to decline, neuroscientists are increasingly researching scans representing the more desirable sensations associated with pleasure and joy.

For idealists, consciousness is the totality of how we perceive and interact qualitatively with the world and each other. Rather than an unproven, magical 'emergence' of conscious qualities resulting from complex neural activity, they argue that mental perceptions *are made up of* consciousness and *take place in* consciousness. In Kastrup's words, "all things and phenomena can be explained as excitations of consciousness itself."

Using the VR game analogy, these 'excitations of consciousness' would be akin to the different possible configurations of bits and bytes that generate the stimuli and gameplay on the screen of perception in a multiplayer online video game. These countless configurations depend on the players' interactions with the game's software code and with each other. In this analogy, the software code of the VR game would constitute the 'physical' laws as the ruleset of the game.

Kastrup talks about consciousness as being the thing that leads to our subjective experiences and likens it to ripples in an ocean. Ripples are made up of water. You can have water without ripples, but the idea of ripples without water is nonsense.

Similarly, our thoughts and experiences can be thought of as ripples in the ocean of greater consciousness.

In Kastrup's metaphor, our individual personal awareness (our 'self' if you will) is akin to a whirlpool within the ocean of consciousness. A temporary disturbance of the whole, causing a limited 'dissociated' perspective. We move around within the ocean, touching other whirlpools and generating more and more ripples.

Many of us are so indoctrinated into the materialist worldview that this feels like a substantial leap of faith. The idea that our brains and bodies are *within* consciousness, rather than consciousness *resulting* from complex brain activity, initially seems to be a convoluted answer to a question we're not certain needed to be asked. If this is the case for you, it's worthwhile following Kastrup's crash course on analytical idealism[1].

But what about our subconscious?

One of the questions many people have about the whirlpool metaphor for human consciousness is how it can account for our unconscious or subconscious drives. The idea of the subconscious was first put forward by Freud, but almost no one would now contest the idea that there are things within our own minds that influence us but that we may not notice or be able to put into words.

The confusion occurs because both philosophy and psychoanalysis have chosen to use the word "consciousness," but they mean dramatically different things by it.

When we say that something is subconscious or unconscious, we don't actually mean that it's not a part of our consciousness. We mean that it's something that we're not representing linguistically. This might be because we don't know it's there because it's too traumatic for us to acknowledge, or because we don't have the right kind of language to make sense of it with words.

For clarity in the areas of consciousness research, it might have been helpful if Freud had chosen a different term, such as "sub-aware" or "unaware", but sadly, both philosophy and psychotherapy are content to use their terminology as they have historically and we are left to deal with the resulting confusion.

The hardest of hard sciences: Quantum physics and questions of consciousness

Of course, it's not unreasonable to remain unconvinced by arguments put forward by philosophers, however well-reasoned and compelling they may be. We live in a world that values the evidence of science, and particularly the 'hard' sciences, far more than logic and reason.

What makes Kastrup's arguments compelling is that they are also finding support from across the scientific spectrum.

Let's start by looking at one of the 'hardest' of the hard sciences. Physics has historically been seen as the most materialist of the sciences, but advances in quantum physics (and more recently, quantum biology) lend substantial support to an idealist view of the world.

You are probably familiar with at least some of the conversations around quantum physics. Discussion of Schroedinger's cat has entered the general conversation, though the ideas behind it are rarely accurately understood.

The most interesting finding (for us) from quantum physics is the discovery that much of the world around us changes when we observe it. Most of us are not surprised that people sense when they are observed. We can imagine how we might respond to being observed, and consider a wide variety of changes we might make to our behavior under those circumstances. Nevertheless, discovering that quantum particles also respond to being observed requires a different level of explanation, however.

If we consider the whirlpool analogy we introduced above, it's possible to apply the same explanation to both situations. An observer is a whirlpool in the oceanic stream of consciousness, creating ripples by the very nature of their vortex' existence. When an observer observes another person (another whirlpool or vortex in the stream of consciousness), their ripples make contact with the outer edge of that person's whirlpool. This creates change. As the whirlpools and ripples interact, they either reinforce each other or phase out. If that's too abstract for you, imagine a girl staring at a boy on the playground. Either the boy picks up on her stare and interprets it or he doesn't.

Quantum particles could be represented in the whirlpool metaphor by tiny ripples in the oceanic stream of consciousness, untethered to any particular whirlpool. In our less abstract "staring girl" metaphor, one might imagine cloudy weather hanging over the playground casting a shadow over the girl.

Ripples caused by our observations meet the 'natural' ripples, with the unpredictable consequences described by quantum physics: our playground boy might reinterpret the girl's stare as a ray of sunlight suddenly highlights her beautiful smile.

But the nature of the water being "rippled" never changes and remains the essence of the entire ocean, connecting all ripples, currents, and whirlpools.

Another fascinating area of physics that you may have heard of and that offers support for an idealist perspective on the world is quantum entanglement. This is where two (or more) electrons become deeply linked. Once they are entangled, they will both have the exact same quantum state no matter how far apart they are from each other. This has been demonstrated at distances of over 1,000 kilometers.

Entanglement makes little sense in a materialist worldview. How could a change to one object influence another object instantaneously and without any means to communicate between them? Even Einstein had trouble grasping quantum entanglement, referring to it as "spooky action at a distance".

Within our idealist perspective, however, the connection between the two objects is much more intuitive if we consider our VR game analogy. If two 'objects' on the screen of perception appear far apart from each other, we have no problem understanding that these objects are not actually physically separated but mere pixels representing virtual objects on a screen. Some prominent physicists theorize that our entire universe is some sort of holographic projection, a hypothesis that might eventually support a quantum theory of gravity.

If we consider Kastrup's whirlpool metaphor, ripples big or small influence the oceanic stream of consciousness much like the butterfly effect. What's important to take away from these metaphors is that, for idealists, the hologram, VR, or stream of consciousness isn't bound by our intuitive understanding of location, much like the earth as a spherical globe was not intuitive for our ancestors, who only experienced flat horizons. The ripples of our individual whirlpools can reach further than we expect, and, as we shall explore shortly, we may be closer to other people in consciousness than we are in terms of geography.

Psychology and psychoanalysis: More than just your dreams

It's not just recent theories and evidence that offer support for some kind of 'ocean of consciousness'. As far back as 1909, Jung (a follower of Freud, who substantially developed and extended his work) put forward the suggestion of a 'collective unconscious'.

When we talk about Jung's 'collective unconscious', remember that "unconscious" in the field of psychoanalysis actually means "unaware" (as opposed to completely "unconscious" in the medical sense). From the view of the philosophy of consciousness, we might refer to it as a "collective, sub-awareness consciousness" (although that hardly trips off the tongue) or, as Kastrup does, the 'mind at large'. I like to think of it as our implicit memory: the shared meaning we spontaneously attach to information presented on our sensory screen of perception.

The idea of Jung's collective unconscious came, in part, from the observation that there are many 'archetypes' that appear across all human cultures and within all societies.

For Jung, the collective unconscious was part of the psyche that did not owe its existence to personal experience. While the personal unconscious is made up essentially of contents that have at one time been conscious but which have disappeared from consciousness through having been forgotten or repressed, the contents of the collective unconscious have never been individually acquired, but owe their existence exclusively to heredity. Noam Chomsky prefers the term "inherited genetic endowment".

Whereas the personal unconscious consists for the most part of complexes (behavior or beliefs copied from the social environment during childhood), the content of the collective unconscious is made up essentially of 'archetypes'. Archetypes can be considered metaphors for deeply rooted concepts or notions that humans all seem to share without requiring explicit learning. Most of these shared notions come to life in different symbols or characters, typically shaped by evolving cultural bias throughout history. The interesting part is that, although they may appear as slightly different symbols in different cultures, at the core of these concepts, there is a universal commonality and meaning we understand intuitively.

Here are a few examples of Jungian archetypes:

- The **Mother**: We come into this world ready to want a mother or a mother substitute. The mother archetype is our built-in ability to recognize a certain relationship (a nurturing-one). We project the archetype, usually onto our own mother, and we tend to personify the archetype by turning it into a mythological "story-book" character, symbolized as "earth mother," Eve and Mary in western traditions, and by less personal symbols such as the church, the nation, a forest, or the ocean.

- The **Shadow**: Sex and life instincts are part of the shadow, which is derived from our prehuman, animal past, when our concerns were limited to survival and reproduction. It is the "dark side" of the ego, and the evil that we are capable of is often stored there. The shadow is amoral, neither good nor bad, just like animals. An animal is capable of both tender care for its young and vicious killing for food, but it doesn't choose to do either. It just does what it does. The shadow becomes something of a garbage can for the parts of ourselves that we can't quite admit to. Symbols of the shadow include the snake (as in the garden of Eden), the dragon, monsters, and demons. It often guards the entrance to a cave or a pool of water, which is the collective unconscious. Next time you dream about wrestling with the devil, it may only be yourself you are wrestling with!

- The **Persona** represents our public image. The fiction is presented in the manner in which we prefer it to appear. The persona relates to the words, person, and personality, and comes from the Latin word for mask. So, the persona is the mask you put on before you show yourself to the outside world. At its best, it is just the "good impression" we all wish to present as we fill the roles society requires of us. But, it can also be the "false impression" we use to manipulate people's opinions and behaviors. At its worst, it can be mistaken, even by ourselves, for our true nature: sometimes we believe we really are what we pretend to be.

- The male (**Animus**) and female (**Anima**) archetypes that we must play are a part of our persona. For most people, that role is determined by their physical gender. However, Jung and others believed that we are all bisexual by nature. We begin as fetuses without differentiated sex organs, but then hormones make us male or female, and our social lives begin as infants mold us into men and women. Jung felt that societal expectations meant that we had developed only half of our potential. The anima and animus together are referred to as a **syzygy**. The anima may be personified as a young girl, very spontaneous and intuitive, as a witch, or as the earth mother. The animus may be personified as a wise old

man, a sorcerer, or a number of males, and tends to be logical and rationalistic.
- The **Child**, child god, or child-hero: the Christ child, celebrated at Christmas, is a child archetype that represents the future, becoming, rebirth, and salvation.
- Story characters, like the **Hero** -defeater of evil dragons, basically represent the ego and are often engaged in fighting the shadow in the form of dragons and monsters. The hero is often as dumb as a post. He is ignorant of the ways of the collective unconscious. The hero is frequently on the prowl for the **Maiden**, whose purity and innocence he admires.
- The **Trickster**- represented by a clown or magician- role is to hamper the hero's progress.

Jung's interpretation is that these archetypes commonly speak to us because they represent part of our 'collective unconscious', which is intuitively accessible to us at a subconscious level. Many marketing agencies still use the Jungian archetype framework today to profile and develop archetypical brands.

Figure 2

Jung saw our development as individuals, known as individuation, as the process of identifying which parts of the collective unconscious we identify with, and spinning them into a coherent narrative befitting our sense of personality.

Individuation is a developmental stage that occurs throughout childhood, but is particularly acute during the teenage years and very early adulthood. Much of the rebellion associated with teenage children is actually the process of individuation resolving itself. Young childhood, before individuation, can be thought of as the gestation of our psyche. Individuation is then analogous to birth. Returning to Kastrup's whirlpool metaphor, one might argue it's the moment when ripples and currents have collided to create a new vortex.

As you might imagine, while children are engaging in the process of individuation, they are particularly vulnerable to outside influences. Just as each of us is never more vulnerable than we were at the time of our birth, our personality and our psyche are never more vulnerable than during individuation, a time when ripples have an increased chance of spinning our whirlpools out of control.

As you think of the average teenager experiencing and engaging with individuation, the danger becomes clear. At the exact moment that they are most mentally and emotionally vulnerable, they are also subject to increasing influence from advertisers.

For Jung, the goal of life was to realize the self, another archetype that represents the transcendence of all natural opposites, so that every aspect of a personality is expressed equally. The moment when you feel neither and both male and female, neither and both ego and shadow, neither and both good and bad, neither and both conscious and unconscious, neither and both an individual and the whole of creation. With no opposites, there is no energy and you cease to act. Of course, you no longer need to act.

To keep it from getting too mystical, think of it as a new center, a more balanced position for the psyche. When we are young, we focus on the ego and worry about the trivialities of the persona. When we get older (assuming we've been developing as we should), we focus a little deeper on ourselves, and become closer to all people, all life, and even the universe itself. In other words, a self-realized person is less selfish.

Brain development and neuroscience

When we look at Jung's work in the context of contemporary neuroscience, we start to develop a picture of the overall predicament our children are in. Young children have developing brains that will adapt to the environment they experience.

When we talk about young children's brains adapting to the world around them, we often imagine that these changes will be minor. We expect incremental change because we assume that some fundamental things can simply not be changed.

For example, we can understand that children may have shorter attention spans if they are always presented with lots of distractions and exciting stimuli. That makes intuitive sense to us. As does the idea that their language development could be accelerated or delayed as a result of the way we interact with them. Again, we can see a logical connection, and the change seems reasonable.

But what if I were to tell you that the wrong kind of upbringing could lead your child's brain to be unable to process vertical lines? That they could have nothing wrong with their eyes, but they would never "see" vertical lines because their brains couldn't process them. And that this could happen without any injury or 'brain damage', simply by controlling the information they see. This will probably stretch your credulity, but it's true.

Admittedly, researchers haven't tested this on children (thankfully!), but it is a very famous experiment that has been conducted on animals and shown to be consistent. Semir Zeki, a neurobiologist who's optimistic about the prospects of bringing the brain sciences to augment creativity in the visual arts (a precursor to advertising), nevertheless reminds us that "how the brain combines the responses of specialized cells to indicate a continuous vertical line is a mystery that neurology has not yet solved." If animals are kept in an environment with no vertical lines, their brains lose the ability to "see" something vertical. Similarly, if they were shown no horizontally, they would retain the ability to see vertically, but not horizontal lines. These animal experiments support the thought experiment about a blind physicist who knows 'the whole of physics' but is confined to a black-and-white room, preventing her from experiencing the quality or sensation of color: According to Chomsky, this fictitious physicist not only lacks the knowledge of the world we live in (as in knowing-*how* or knowing-*that*), but also lacks "knowledge *of* – knowledge of rules and principles that yield unbounded capacities to act appropriately but may remain inaccessible to consciousness".

More importantly, after a certain developmental stage, such experimental changes are irreversible (although with technological advances, who knows what might be possible in the future), which warrants extra caution in the (virtual) environments we submerge our children into.

Of course, there are also incredible examples of mind over matter on the opposite side of the spectrum, like the extreme nurturing of child intuition to beat the odds in clairvoyance, to name one. Anomalies in this pioneering area of consciousness research are often prematurely dismissed at the risk of career suicide, touching on anything even tangentially 'psi' related.

When we talk throughout this book about the risks to young children and their developing brains, I would like you to remember the real magnitude of the impact we are talking about. Limiting their environment can lead to them being literally incapable of seeing things that we know are objectively present.

This may also help if you are finding some of the more theoretical aspects of this chapter difficult to accept. If we are not shown something in our environment as we are developing, we may become literally 'blind' to it. Just because we can't see something doesn't mean it's not there.

To a certain extent, the opposite also appears to hold for children who have been supported (instead of discouraged or even punished) in their belief that they can do virtually anything they put their (intuitive) minds to.

Morphic resonance and morphic fields

Further support for an idealist way of approaching the world comes from a new generation of biologists that follow in the trailblazing footsteps of Dr. Rupert Sheldrake, one of the few brave scientific pioneers that suffered the wrath of academic taboo on the count of engaging in "psi" related research.

Mr. Sheldrake pointed to a wide variety of phenomena across biology, including both animal behavior and even plant growth, that point to a form of intangible memory shared across different organisms, even when they have no contact with (or influence over) each other in the material world.

Sheldrake refers to this shared memory as morphic resonance, and suggests that the more closely linked different entities are, the more powerful the morphic resonance is.

As a memory of the past, morphic resonance can be thought of as a link between individuals through time. He also provides evidence that suggests a morphic link between individuals in the present.

Sheldrake calls these present-moment links 'morphic fields'. If you've ever wondered, for example, how it is that your dog always seems to know when you're on your way home, Sheldrake has a suggestion. He's carried out intricate experiments to remove any other potential cues (sometimes known as 'demand characteristics'). Even without a reliable time of arrival or any associated sights or sounds, Fido does seem to know when we're nearly back and is ready to greet us. Sheldrake offers morphic fields as the only remaining explanation.

I hope that the parallels between Sheldrake's morphic fields and whirlpools in an ocean of consciousness are apparent. Morphic resonance can also fit well into this metaphor, as ripples can remain in the ocean of consciousness to influence those who come after us, even long after the vortex of our whirlpool dissolves.

What does this mean for my child's development?

By now, I am sure that some readers will be wondering how any of this relates to either the rise of neuromarketing or protecting our children. I'm grateful for your indulgence.

I mentioned earlier, one of the most radical changes we need to make is in how we think about the world. When we are trying to create solutions to one of the most serious and intractable problems that face us today, it's important to realize that we're not working alone.

Our thoughts, our beliefs, and our experiences will guide the solutions that we are willing to accept, but they also connect us to others. Widespread social change comes about when large groups of people start thinking about the same thing and try to approach it in a similar way.

This is part of a phenomenon known as emotional contagion. Imagine spending time with someone who is particularly anxious, or desperately happy. How do you feel after spending a day or a week with them? Most of us will find that we have absorbed some portion of their emotions. Our ripples have changed as a result of our interactions with them.

It has been suggested that the Summer of Love was an example of emotional contagion. Although there were a few prominent locations, people across much of the world found that they were sharing intense feelings of love, goodwill, affection, trust, and a desire for freedom.

A more recent, though less positive, example might be the COVID pandemic or geopolitical nuclear threats. In the midst of global crises, almost all of us feel our anxiety levels rising. We also pick up on the anxiety of others, and they pick up on ours. The ripples of fear spread across the world. These ripples can be originated by one relatively small whirlpool in the consciousness ocean that manages to either synchronize with other whirlpools to create a new current or tide, or in some rare cases, even impact the core structure of our vortices.

If our solutions are to be successfully implemented, we will need to work together, to create intellectual as well as emotional contagion, and to create ripples that become a huge wave. Because if we allow advertising to continue to affect our children's development in the way it currently is, we might find that the underlying currents in the ocean of consciousness are changing, and not for the better.

Chapter 3
Trends in (consumer) neuroscience

"The problem with market research is that people don't think how they feel, they don't say what they think, and they don't do what they say."

- David Ogilvy

Chapter 3 Executive Summary:

- The advertising sector is increasingly adopting insights from brain scanning and bio-sensor feedback technology previously used only by the academic and medical research communities.
- A mainstream adoption of consumer neuroscience and neuromarketing technology

triggers ethical concerns about the use of highly intimate consumer information being available only to marketers and not the consumers themselves.
- Artificial intelligence algorithms, designed to maximize the advertisers' financial profits, will boost the effects of neuromarketing before the social ramifications have been thoroughly investigated.
- Regulators are paralyzed by the overwhelming task of trying to keep up with sector innovations and finding the right balance between advertiser and consumer interests.

What is neuromarketing?

We've already talked a little bit about neuromarketing in Chapter 1. In this chapter, we're going to take a more in-depth look at the different neuromarketing techniques currently in use. It's important that we understand the techniques that are available to companies, what they are trying to achieve by using them, and why this is more than just an incremental change from the past.

Of course, advertisers and marketing professionals have always used any tools available to them to achieve the results they're looking for. To say that it is a competitive market is an enormous understatement. Even a slight edge can make all the difference to a marketing campaign, and hence to the company it serves. The market for 'AdTech' or 'MarTech' is flooded with new tech startups developing apps and tools to help advertisers with their attempt to better connect with the consumer and grow their market (share).

Where did neuromarketing techniques come from?

The technologies we are going to look at have come directly from medical and scientific research conducted in universities and research centers around the world. These tools have been used by academics to understand how the brain works since the dawn of modern advertising in the 1920s.

Each tool has been devised to tell us something different about how the brain processes information. Some are focused on which areas of the brain are active during a particular activity, while others show us a clear picture of when the brain is active during different stages of a task.

Some of these are cheap to run and easy to work with. Others, for example, fMRI, are prohibitively expensive for now. As always, technology becomes more affordable as time passes.

Let's look at the major neuroscience research tools that are now being used to inform neuromarketing agencies. There are many different tools out there but we're going to look at the most important, and the most widely used ones.

The powerful tools being adopted by the advertising industry

If we're going to talk about the risks of neuromarketing, we really need to understand the techniques. At the very least, we need to understand what the most common tools are able to achieve and whether there are any constraints on their use. The tools we are going to look at are fMRI, EEG, eye-tracking, pupillometry, and biometrics. It could be argued that biometrics aren't strictly *neuro*marketing tools because they measure physical responses more generally. While this might be true from an academic or linguistic perspective, they are often used in conjunction with other neuromarketing tools and are used to acquire the same kinds of information.

You might be wondering how it's possible to reconcile the power of techniques based on brain imaging with the philosophical idealism that we described previously. It's actually very straightforward. Brain activity is associated with changes in your state of consciousness, but that doesn't mean that your neurons *cause* these changes. Kastrup observes that brain activity is the observable manifestation of our "whirlpool's" disturbance caused by an external ripple, like an advertisement. As such, brain scans provide highly relevant insights into the impact a single ad can have. They allow us to study commonalities and turn insights based on neural correlates of consciousness into applications that promise ever more predictable (consumer) behavior.

fMRI

Functional magnetic resonance imaging (fMRI) is a powerful tool to help us understand exactly which regions of the brain are working harder when we are presented with a specific advertisement or asked to make a particular decision.

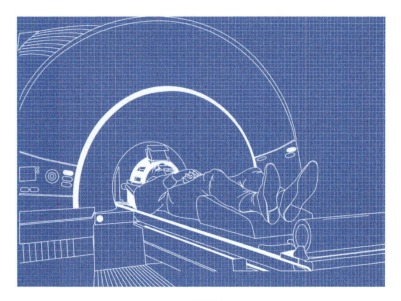

Figure 3 (MRI Blueprints)

It uses an MRI scanner to measure how much blood is going to specific brain regions. Areas that are working harder need more oxygen, and so will demand higher blood flow. If we are able to locate the areas with higher-than-normal blood flow, we can infer that they are actively processing information at that point in time.

The word 'functional' in fMRI highlights that we are taking many scans over a short period of time, which allows us to measure the changes throughout a task.

If research talks about specific brain areas being activated, they will *usually* be talking about fMRI.

Of all of the techniques we are going to talk about here, fMRI is probably the most powerful, and also the least used. MRI machines are huge, incredibly expensive pieces of machinery that are typically found in hospitals and major research institutions. For context, there are probably only about 12,000 MRI machines in the entirety of the United States and around 36,000 globally.

They also ask a lot of the people participating in the research. Members of the public are asked to lie very still in a moderately claustrophobic and very noisy environment.

An fMRI study can help companies to understand how customers are responding to products, pricing, and advertisements, and is also useful for exploring ideas around brand loyalty and emotional responses to specific offerings.

The state of the art in fMRI-based consumer neuroscience has developed to a stage where we can now reconstruct your mental representation of a commercial movie based solely on the readouts of your fMRI recordings taken whilst watching the movie.

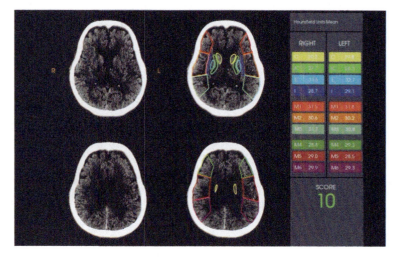

Figure 4

EEG

EEG stands for electroencephalogram (a piece of information that probably doesn't help you to understand what it does and how it works). If you've ever seen pictures of experiments where someone is wearing what looks like a swim cap with lots of little wires coming out of it, that's an EEG.

EEG relies on the fact that brain cells responding to something will all fire at the same time. This can best be summarized as "neurons that fire together, wire together". This creates a big enough electrical charge that can be measured from your scalp.

Spacing the electrodes all over the scalp gives researchers some idea about which brain areas are active, but it's *much* less precise (in terms of location) than fMRI. The main benefit of EEG is that it responds incredibly quickly, allowing us to pick up on very small changes in brain activity that occur for a tiny period of time. This allows it to be very precise about *when* brain activity takes place.

Taking part in an EEG experiment is significantly less of a burden than an fMRI experiment, but we're still asking for a significant investment of time and energy from research participants. Most EEG experiments take over an hour, and researchers often complain that the people they were studying actually fell asleep part-way through the experiment!

EEG gives researchers a millisecond-by-millisecond picture of how the brain is responding to what customers are seeing and experiencing. Using this information, companies can understand exactly what we're paying attention to, what attracts our attention, and what allows us to become distracted, especially in combination with eye-tracking (see below). High temporal precision (e.g. capturing a significant electrical brain discharge exactly 400 milliseconds after displaying a brand stimulus) brings the promise of tapping into the subconscious consumer mind. The latter represents the holy grail for marketers, as instinctive, subconscious associations are claimed to drive up to 95% of consumers' consideration sets.

The state of the art in EEG-based (medical) neuroscience has evolved to the extent that we can already reconstruct non-vocalized, imagined speech based on intracranial EEG (currently used by patients with severe epilepsy). Commercial grade EEG headsets that will be able to decode the consumer's subconscious 'inner speech' when processing branded sensory information will hit the 'Alternative Augmentative Communication' (AAC) market in a matter of years.

Eye-tracking

Eye-tracking (or, more specifically, gaze-tracking) software does pretty much exactly what it sounds like. Customers are shown images on a screen, and hidden cameras record where they are looking at any particular moment.

You might think that we know where we are looking, and that this wouldn't reveal anything particularly interesting. In reality, our eyes move far more than we notice and offer a lot of useful information about our attention and our preferences. For obvious reasons, marketers want to know which visual aspects of their ads are capturing attention, and in which order. This research is typically referred to as a 'heatmap'.

Your eyes are never still. As you're reading this book, they will be making micro-movements called saccades. Your eyes dance around your visual world, but they return more often to things you are paying attention to.

The main drawback for marketers when it comes to heatmaps is that, in and of themselves, they are unable to reveal what consumers are thinking when they gaze at a specific aspect of an ad.

Where fMRI and EEG offer companies insight into our emotional responses to an aspect of their marketing, eye-tracking offers information about how and where we direct our attention, and more importantly, how this changes in response to different types of advertising.

Importantly, eye-tracking can offer companies more informed assumptions based on the information we are paying at least some attention to than we could ourselves without using this objective measuring technique. As I have mentioned previously, we're often unaware of the full scope of information our brains have taken in and processed.

Eye-tracking software offers a dramatically more accurate measure of the focus (and breadth) of our attention than self-reported studies.

Figure 5

Pupillometry

Pupillometry is the measurement of how dilated our pupils are. This could possibly be considered a part of biometrics (see below), but biometric research tends to use a variety of different measurements in one study to gain meaningful results. Pupilometry, on the other hand, tends to be used as a stand-alone measure.

You're probably familiar with the idea that your pupils dilate when you look at someone you're attracted to. In fact, they will dilate when you are feeling almost any strong emotion and when you are having to work hard to understand and process information.

A major challenge for marketers when considering this technique is that emotional responses are hyper-personal. Just because your pupils start to dilate when being exposed to a sexy Tinder ad doesn't mean that your neighbor will have the same emotional reaction.

Pupilometry, therefore, can give us a measure of the intensity of someone's emotional responses (although it won't tell us which emotion). It can also highlight when people are confused or have to put extra effort into understanding a message.

Figure 6

Biometrics

The term 'biometrics' is appearing everywhere at the moment, from passport designs to how you unlock your phone. That's not surprising when you realize that it literally means "measuring something about your body". Technically, jumping on the weight scale in the morning counts as biometrics.

When we talk about biometrics from a neuromarketing perspective, we're talking about measuring changes in the way your skin conducts electricity (known as galvanic skin response, or GSR), your blood pressure, and how fast your heart is beating, for example.

These are essentially the same measurements used in a lie detector or polygraph test, and we're looking for pretty much the same things. Polygraph tests work because almost all of us feel some form of stress when we tell a lie. Measuring the way our bodies react in such minute detail allows scientists to identify that stress response, and therefore detect a lie.

Biometric studies in neuromarketing aren't about telling when we're lying, but recording those tiny changes that signal changes in your emotional response, including fear, happiness, surprise, or disgust.

Facial analysis is an emotion research methodology that uses electronic sensors to detect subtle and not-so-subtle muscle movements in the face. These movements supposedly correlate with a respondent's emotional reactions to a stimulus.

Figure 7 - Facial analysis is an emotion research methodology that uses electronic sensors to detect subtle and not-so-subtle muscle movements in the face. These movements supposedly correlate with a respondent's emotional reactions to a stimulus.

Isn't this just more of the same?

As we've examined the different techniques used by neuromarketers, there have been some common themes. The information they're gaining is all about what we're paying attention to and how we think and feel. But, we've always known that marketing and advertising departments care about what attracts our attention and how we feel about products. This raises the question as to whether there's anything fundamentally different about neuromarketing compared with older research techniques.

The answer is very clear. The areas of interest are the same, but neuromarketing takes things to a whole new level. It also raises some very clear ethical concerns, which were concerning enough to lead France to ban the use of brain imaging in marketing in 2004.

With neuromarketing, companies are able to ask questions that we ourselves don't know the answers to, and obtain the answers they are looking for from our physiological responses. In some cases, the results they obtain will be diametrically opposed to the answers we would give if asked directly.

In some cases, this will be a reflection of our underlying emotional responses without the filters of social expectations, acceptability, and social responsibility that we place on ourselves. For example, if a vegan is presented with a bacon sandwich, they might verbally (and honestly) express disgust. Neuromarketing techniques, on the other hand, might reveal a whole host of other emotions and responses, including hunger and pleasure.

If neuromarketing can access those parts of ourselves that we would rather not acknowledge, even to ourselves, how does that translate to the mass processing of marketing messaging that we are continuously bombarded with below conscious awareness? How comfortable are we with that highly intimate information being available only to marketers and not to ourselves? And, shouldn't the social constraints we put on ourselves also be important and valued when making marketing decisions? Surely, they should play a key role in guiding new ethical industry standards.

What would an advertising ecosystem that was driven solely by underlying desires and unfettered by social expectations and moral restraint look like?

I'd rather the answer to that question stay firmly in the realms of science fiction.

It's worth highlighting here that I'm not advocating banning all neuromarketing techniques. Technology is not the enemy. It's about making sure that we have the right types of education and regulation to ensure that it's used responsibly and ethically.

The rise of AI in neuromarketing

We're going to talk in more depth in the next chapter about some of the newer neuromarketing techniques that are still in the early stages of their development, and that make greater use of AI.

We do need to acknowledge that the rise of AI in neuromarketing (and, realistically, in almost all areas of advertising) is inevitable. But the rise of AI doesn't have to be the Rise of the Machines.

One of the most important things to understand about AI is that it has no inherent moral value. AI isn't benevolent, nor is it malign. It's fast and it's powerful, but it's driven by us. If our traditional techniques are akin to traveling on foot, then, AI is like riding a racehorse. We're still responsible for the destination, but we'll get there much faster. And as anyone who's ridden horses (or tried to develop AI software) will attest, there will probably also be a few unplanned diversions en route.

One of the concerns around AI technologies at the moment is that they are being driven by software designers and coders; people coming predominantly from a STEM[1] background. Coding solutions are required for AI problems that are couched as technological problems. Coders frequently share the same rational values and may overlook the implications of their developments on people who have had very different, perhaps more human-centric backgrounds than they do.

This is exacerbated by the purpose behind the technology. The algorithms are being created and refined to maximize profit, without any real motivation to consider the social ramifications. This raises concerns not only about the current use of AI but also about the direction of future developments.

AI and cognitive neuroscience in our daily lives: Powerful tools, incredible results

AI and cognitive neuroscience are already having a significant impact on the world around us. They're incredibly powerful tools being used in a huge range of areas of our lives. In many ways, this is great news, but it's a source of concern. The more powerful these technologies are, the greater their ability to affect our lives, for better or for worse.

Cognitive neuroscience is being used to help us understand ourselves, and to help find treatments for a wide range of different disorders. These include complex, poorly-understood conditions such as Autism Spectrum

Disorder, as well as those we understand quite well but have struggled to find effective treatments for, such as Parkinson's disease.

In the world of work, cognitive neuroscience is increasingly being used to create training around diversity, equity, and inclusion, as well as effective negotiation. Indeed, cognitive neuroscience in combination with natural language processing (a niche within AI) is used to inform and train FBI hostage negotiators. The stakes don't get much higher than that!

AI is similarly becoming a part of our everyday lives. Mostly, this is taking the form of machine learning (ML). It's probably fair to say that AI and ML are at the center of the majority of significant innovations coming out at the moment, for everything from self-driving cars to reducing racial bias in recruitment.

One of the most powerful applications of ML is in diagnosing serious illnesses. Although we might value the personal touch of visiting our personal physician, we are likely to get a more accurate diagnosis if we outsource the decision to AI.

If this piques your interest, I'd strongly suggest checking out 'Noise' by Daniel Kahneman. Cognitive neuroscience and AI are exciting, giving us ideas how to reduce undesired variability in human judgment. They're also not toys. They are powerful tools that will play an increasing role in *professional* human judgments that affect your life, and we must use them with caution. We wouldn't give our teenagers the keys to a Lamborghini before they'd passed Drivers' Ed (or indeed, afterward, but that's beside the point). Similarly, we need to consider what rules need to be in place for safeguarding creativity and diversity as companies take increasing advantage of these techniques.

The growth of neuromarketing: A slower-than-expected revolution

It's important to note that the growth of neuromarketing hasn't been quite as rapid as many of us might have expected. There are several reasons for this.

One of the most obvious explanations is that the tools discussed so far only really provide greater detail and nuance to the information they already had available, at substantially greater cost. Few businesses will be willing or able to spend tens of thousands of dollars on an fMRI study to confirm the accuracy of their focus group findings..

The huge costs associated with research can only really become acceptable to a company's bottom line when they reach a certain size and scale. This often rules out start-ups and smaller or more local companies.

Some companies may also have concerns about attracting the attention of regulators or receiving negative publicity. At the moment, this type of research isn't really subject to high levels of oversight or even simple curiosity from members of the public. They may be unsure as to how their customers might respond to discovering the sophistication of their research methods, and so limit the use of more innovative techniques.

If neuromarketing presents a slight risk, while only offering marginal returns, it's not surprising that companies are slow to jump on the bandwagon. This slow, steady growth is a predictable phase, and we are expecting some form of innovation or new application in the next few years that will lead to an explosion in the use of neuromarketing, far beyond its current levels. In the next chapter, we are going to look at a potential candidate for new and emerging neuromarketing, and what it could mean.

Regulators: late to the party, or uninvited guests?

The techniques we have outlined in this chapter have only recently come to be used in the areas of advertising and marketing, and their use hasn't been widely publicized outside of academic or industry circles.

There's nothing sinister about that fact. How many of us (outside of the industry) talk about market research tools over breakfast? Unfortunately, it does mean that two important groups of stakeholders aren't sufficiently aware of what's going on; consumers and politicians.

We're going to talk in much more detail about the importance of making consumers aware of how marketing works, and the tools being used to understand and manipulate them in Chapter 8. The more we, as consumers, understand the behind-the-scenes processes, the better we are able to protect ourselves and make good decisions.

It's also essential that those working in regulation are also sufficiently aware of the threats posed by current practices, and that they have the authority to question (and halt) new developments where they pose a risk.

Regulating is a difficult task, which requires a delicate balance between supporting innovation (and avoiding any unnecessary burdens on vulnerable start-ups) and protecting consumers and society at large.

Regulators can only work within the framework they have been given by our politicians, which is why they are often slow to respond to new challenges. If politicians are unaware of the concerns neuromarketing techniques can (and sometimes should) raise, regulators will be hamstrung in their efforts to take companies to task for questionable practices.

Neuromarketing is developing rapidly, and we need a public discussion to make sure that we all understand where we are, where the technology is going, and what limits we can or should have on these emerging technologies.

Chapter 4
Advanced techniques in consumer neuroscience

"It takes a long time to educate intuition. Clearly AI is going to win. How people are going to adjust is a fascinating problem."

- Daniel Kahneman

Chapter 4 Executive Summary:

- Consumers don't stand much chance in resisting modern day advertising strategies. Advertisers being able to accurately predict human emotions and related behavioral responses are limiting our free will below conscious awareness.
- The progression of neuromarketing technology

into a deeply unethical space is not inevitable. We need to educate consumers to prevent the worst case scenarios.
- Unintentional neuromarketing side-effects are particularly alarming for children, whose belief systems are still developing and who are more susceptible to emotional nudges.
- Individual Big-Tech CEO biases are cemented in the core of the artificial intelligence algorithms driving social media recommendation engines.

The holy grail of marketing: Finding the "buying" button in your brain

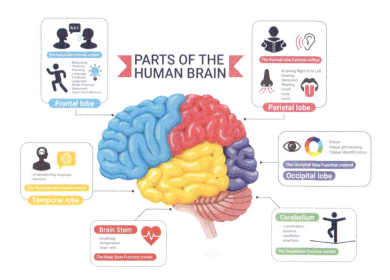

Figure 8 - Functional areas of the brain. Advertisers are trying to decode the "buy button" in the brain.

So far, we've been looking at how established techniques originally developed for academic or medical research have been used by companies to refine their advertising and marketing efforts.

Although the integration of some of these techniques has been slower than we might expect, the tide is clearly moving further and further in this direction, and the developments are picking up pace.

As companies become accustomed to having increasingly sophisticated information about us, our attention, and our emotions, it's not surprising that they are keen to know more. Especially if this can be achieved without the need for bulky medical equipment and costly experiments.

If you try to imagine the ideal neuromarketing technique from the perspective of a company, you might imagine a tool that allows easy access to a substantial proportion of their customer base (and especially to potential customers who have not yet interacted with their brand). It would require a minimal expenditure, and provide information about customers' emotional responses on a moment-by-moment basis. Ideally, customers would have minimal awareness that they were being studied, to avoid them changing their behavior to fulfill social expectations.

This might sound slightly dystopian in terms of privacy, but you can see how it would provide advertisers with the most valuable data possible to guide their decisions. Throughout the rest of this chapter, we're going to examine how possible this really is.

The growth of Big Data, why we weren't worried, and why we were wrong

Concerns about privacy and the amount of data we're making available about ourselves are almost as old as the internet itself. In some ways, it's surprising that these concerns haven't reached the boiling point yet.

Part of the explanation for this is that these concerns were allayed in the mid-to-late 2000s, based on a principle that simply doesn't hold true anymore. In the years shortly after the millennium, privacy campaigners (and interested members of the public) realized that large amounts of complex data were being gathered about all of us, all the time.

When these concerns were raised, the response was always the same. "Yes. We *have* the data, but we can't *use* it." The scale of the information gathered about us was seen as our protection, as well as part of the risk. No one believed that we would be able to actually process that much data to produce meaningful information in a sensible timeframe.

This reduced the sense of urgency felt by members of the public, if not by privacy campaigners. There was a belief that we had time to regulate and legislate before any of our concerns became reality.

That reassurance now seems laughably quaint. Not only do we have the processing capacity to process the enormous amount of intimate behavioral data gathered, many companies are starting to harvest the fruits of their data mining strategies. Our anonymous information is out there, and it can tell companies more than we can possibly imagine.

A picture tells a thousand words. Your online profile tells you all

Until relatively recently, facial recognition software was very much a work in progress. Neural networks were learning to recognize tanks more than a generation ago, but human facial recognition has been a particularly difficult problem to solve, especially from less-than-ideal data. We could train algorithms to match faces from still photographs taken in bright light with identical facial expressions, but this was of little value in real-world settings.

The increased processing power mentioned above, combined with innovative software design, has led to huge improvements in facial recognition software over recent years, including real-time facial recognition scans of everyone in specific public spaces. Undoubtedly, this is a huge technological advance, though you may have some associated privacy concerns.

In tandem with the rise of facial recognition software, there has been a parallel focus on software designed to 'read' our faces. As we become used to having our webcams available more frequently, and even using our faces to unlock our phones, some advertisers are trying to take advantage of our increased familiarity and comfort with the technology. I'm sure you can imagine the value to advertisers of being able to use facial analysis software to understand our emotions whenever we're online.

This work is very much in its infancy, and at the moment, the technology is not able to fulfill the promises some companies offering it are making. But it is just one example of the vast range of data that can easily be collected about us.

The Internet of Things (IoT) is a term used to refer to the way that so many of our products are now internet-enabled, and are constantly gathering information about us and our behavior for user profiling purposes. Home gadgets, from your thermostat to your coffee machine, are increasingly controlled with an app, but the IoT goes far further than that. Miniature sensors that communicate with the app are built into our apparel, furniture, equipment and household utilities (to name a few) in order to feed your online user profile with ever more intimate user data. This continuous stream of contextual information helps predict your behavior with increasing precision and provides a feedback loop to the manufacturers for future product release updates. If Elon Musk's Neuralink vision comes to fruition, miniature sensors will soon be voluntarily injected into our brains to 'unlock' a next generation of consumer applications.

This increased internet connectivity is supposed to improve our quality of life, but it also supposes unprecedented access to our intimate behaviors and habits for marketers.

Intellect or emotions? Advertisers know the answer

When researchers use webcams and facial recognition software to monitor and analyze our reactions, what is it actually telling them? As with many of the neuromarketing techniques mentioned in the previous chapter, they're looking specifically at our emotions.

Initially, this might seem comforting. We're used to the idea that other people can read our emotions from our facial expressions, our tone of voice, our body language, and the words we use.

All that feels much more comfortable than someone being able to read our minds, understand our thoughts, or predict the decisions we are going to make.

The more you think about it, however, the more dangerous it can seem. Our emotions drive our behavior at a fundamental level. Our deepest needs, for example, the need to have a comfortable supply of food and shelter, are closely linked with our emotions. They can fuel a subconscious, yet existential fear that can drive so many of our choices instinctively. Our culturally biased need for social acceptance and success is another example of an underlying emotional driver that often triggers frustration and stress.

We're typically happy to share our thoughts with the people we know. We compare ideas, discuss concepts, and talk about our opinions. Talking about our emotions is often much more personal and even more vulnerable. We never learned to talk explicitly about our feelings. It's even considered taboo for most.

We feel a sense of distance and privacy when we share our thoughts, but that doesn't exist when we share our feelings. If we struggle to trust the people around us with our deepest emotions, are we really happy to allow advertisers and marketers to psychoanalyze them without at least keeping us in the loop of their observations and findings?

And the question can become even more alarming when we consider how they might use that information to make us crave shiny new things that keep our dopamine levels high.

Why is appealing directly to emotions below conscious awareness ethically dubious?

It might go without saying, but appealing to our emotional reactions below our conscious awareness is ethically dubious at best. If AI is able to predict our behavior accurately, and can model hundreds of scenarios in advance to ensure that we make the purchasing decisions they prefer, it raises very real questions about the integrity of the self and our power of free will.

Of course, we *do* still have free will by many definitions, but being able to be accurately predicted and modeled challenges exactly how free we are.

If a stranger approaches us on the street and politely asks for our wallet, we will almost certainly exercise our free will and refuse to hand it over. Let's say that there's a 1% chance that you agree to their request (that's probably a substantial overestimation, but bear with me).

If that same stranger were to demand our wallet and physically threaten us, we would be far more likely to give it to them. Let's suggest that there's a 99% chance that we would obey their demand (at the risk of being shot or stabbed). This is still us exercising our free will, but it's certainly not unconstrained. We have been able to make a decision, but the other person is heavily influencing us in one direction, and we are having to take the consequences into account.

Now imagine a scenario where that same stranger understood us well enough (without us knowing them at all) that they could politely ask with a set of cues or phrases that gave them a 99% chance of walking away with your wallet. How would that make you feel? How constrained is your free will in this scenario?

If you think this is farfetched, I suggest watching the Netflix documentary "The Tinder Swindler".

In the third scenario, there is a huge imbalance of power, and importantly, *we're not aware of it*. We think we're in the first 'polite' scenario, but our behavior is just as constrained as in the second. Based on all the information available to us, we believe that we are making our own decisions based on our personal values, desires, and interests, but this perception is inaccurate. There's still a 1% chance that we will keep our wallet, but our "free will" options feel considerably reduced when someone knows exactly how to push our buttons.

This is remarkably similar to the situation we could find ourselves in if advanced techniques in neuromarketing achieve their full potential.

We, as a society, may come to the conclusion that advertising based entirely on manipulating emotional responses is ethically acceptable, but this hasn't happened yet. At the moment, we're avoiding the conversation entirely. To be genuinely ethical, this debate needs to take place publicly. At least that way, we know which scenario we're in.

Ripples or riptides? How much manipulation is ok?

Again, we can link this back to Kastrup's whirlpool metaphor. According to the analogy, our interactions with the world come through ripples touching the edges of our whirlpool. The ripples make tiny changes to the movement of the water within our whirlpool, but only at the edges. We influence each other through small touches and tiny ripples.

The kind of manipulation that presents a challenge to our free will doesn't just interact gently on the edges of our whirlpool, however. Instead, it frays the very boundaries. This kind of manipulation can be thought of as a huge wave, rather than a small ripple. Of course, our whirlpool will still be there when the wave passes, but it may be diminished or structurally altered in unpredictable ways. If you prefer the virtual reality game metaphor, consider the chance a player has of continuously resisting the countless credits or virtual coins freely up for grabs throughout the entire gameplay.

This research might not actually go anywhere but it could

As always, I do want to emphasize that we certainly haven't reached this position yet. With a little luck (or a lot of effort), we hopefully won't ever get to the stage where we are questioning just how much free will we have been left with.

The progression of this technology into a deeply unethical space is not inevitable. In fact, it risks a paradigm shift in redefining the boundaries of what is actually considered ethical to begin with. This is both the promise and the risk of new and developing technologies. We never know exactly how things are going to turn out. This is why we need to hope for the best but plan for the worst.

The best thing we, as consumers and parents, can do is to keep ourselves informed and think deeply about the implications of any new technology we encounter. We shouldn't shy away from voicing our concerns and contributing to public debate because we feel like helpless David vs. Goliath. Grassroots movements have proven to be agents of major cultural change. We should be asking questions all the time, both of ourselves and of the advertisers and organizations we interact with. If we see something that worries us, we should ask ourselves why it worries us and whether this concern is warranted. If it is, we should then be asking how we can help to fix it. Whether that's by campaigning for regulation or oversight, starting a parents' group, or writing a book to alert other parents to the imminent threat you see around you, take responsibility for taking action.

What does emotionally-oriented marketing mean for our emotionally-ruled children?

As any parent will know, children are fundamentally emotional. They haven't yet developed the intellect and rationality required to make decisions based on reasoning and deliberation. They don't have the self-control needed to delay their personal gratification or to put their current emotional state into a wider perspective.

However inconvenient it might be when a young child has a tantrum in the grocery store, this emotion is a fundamental part of being a child. It's both unavoidable and developmentally necessary. It's also a huge part of what makes childhood so wonderful; being able to respond to the world intuitively, with honest emotions and no filters.

Being so focused on emotions also makes children more vulnerable to emotion-based marketing, however. They lack the intellectual ability to question the messages they are receiving, and are more likely to absorb values, aspirations, and other emotional responses associated with companies and their products.

Even teenagers, widely known for being argumentative and contrary, are profoundly susceptible to this kind of suggestion. In their stage of development, they are trying to understand social rules for themselves, which is why so many are preoccupied with 'fitting in'.

When young people are presented with powerful, emotional messages that they don't have the intellectual capability or nuanced language skills to properly explore, those same messages are accepted implicitly.

Advertising of this kind typically becomes a part of your child's value system. In doing so, it becomes immune from examination and rational questioning. A great deal of psychotherapy involves discovering those emotionally-based beliefs and values absorbed in childhood, and unpacking them from an adult perspective.

the Perfect BrainWash 113

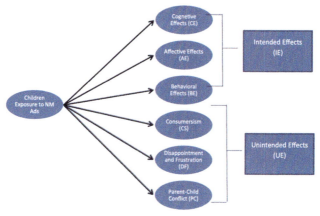

Figure 2: The Theoretical Framework of the Study.

Figure 9 - Source: The Impact of Neuromarketing (NM) Advertising on Children: Intended and Unintended Effects, Amani Al Abbas[1], Weifeng Chen[1], and Maria Saberi[2]

What kind of biases are we cementing into society with this?

It's also worth considering what kinds of biases we are building into our society as we experience these marketing efforts. Marketing both reflects the society we live in and will shape our future community. So what will happen if we continue down the road of increased monitoring of emotional responses, and near-constant exposure to advertising media?

When we talk about advertising cementing in bias, this isn't a deliberate or conscious act. The biases we're talking about here aren't the overt "No Blacks. No Irish" signs from generations ago. Instead, they're aspects of the world that we view as something that "just is", without realizing that it's actually a part of our internalized value system.

Let's take an example from the past. You've probably seen some of the adverts aimed at housewives in the 1950s. They seem both humorous and uncomfortable to us now. We can clearly see the biases they contain, around age, gender, and race. Taken as a relic, they can be comedic, but they can also be a stark warning.

Those ads weren't written with the intention of keeping women in the home or selectively subjugating women of color. They weren't created to effect social change. They were seen as a reflection of natural reality.

When we look at them now, however, we can see the effect that they had; the constant messages that women belong in the home and should be obedient to their husbands. Those messages prevented many women from even considering a different life.

Similar messages could be found around masculine roles as well. The iconic Marlboro Man tobacco adverts used notions of masculinity to sell cigarettes, but they also reaffirmed ideas around what constitutes a "real man".

Advertisers in the 1960s didn't recognize sexism, and so they didn't notice the messages 'hidden' in their work. We're substantially more alert to messaging now, but we can't recognize the messages we don't realize we hold.

No part of our media is 'bias free'. We all have implicit and explicit biases, although we almost certainly don't recognize them as such. Advertising aimed at our emotions solidifies these biases and bypasses our intellectual processes, making it ever easier to pass on powerful social messages.

So, how do we control the biases that our society picks up from advertising? I wish I knew.

Honestly, I suggest that we skip that stage and get right to the root of the problem. We can't eliminate bias, but we can try to keep advertising away from our children until they've had the time to develop a value system of their own against which they can judge the messages they receive. We're going to talk about this more in Chapter 11.

Chapter 5
The "freemium" kiss of death

"If you're not paying for the product, then you are the product"

- Daniel Hövermann.

Chapter 5 Executive Summary:

- Freemium applications are particularly appealing to children who are the most vulnerable to the ads that sponsor the freemium content.
- Social media and mainstream search engines are auctioning our profiles and attention to the highest bidder, regardless of the message advertised.

- Teenagers are spending over 21 hours per week on social media following "influencers", unknown to their parents.
- Current social media AI algorithms reinforce prejudice and addiction.

What is freemium?

One of the biggest revolutions in advertising has been the rise of "freemium" content. In this chapter, we're going to look at what freemium is and the ways in which freemium content uses fundamental psychological techniques to manipulate us. We'll also investigate if these freemium models require regulation in view of ethical concerns or to avoid collateral damage.

Freemium is a business model, where a company provides a basic product or service to users at no cost. The profit comes from users paying for upgrades or premium content and features. It can be found in a wide variety of different areas, such as data storage, music, video streaming, and online gaming.

Although there are many different freemium business models, the basic principle remains constant. Users start with the free, limited service but, over time, will begin to aspire to more and succumb to the allure of the premium service. Or they simply get annoyed with the irritating advertisements nudging them to trade up, just like their peers. At this point, the company begins to charge.

Freemium products aimed largely at children are often games. These games can be completely free to use, but players who buy premium extras will typically win over those players who do not spend real-world money.

These kinds of freemium products typically use emotions such as competitiveness to target users. Some of these games are specifically designed to target young people, taking advantage of their emotion-based decision-making, poor impulse control, and lack of financial awareness. Only a very small minority of users are likely to pay, but they will often spend substantial sums.

Another great example of freemium content is the creative content platforms. Most of the popular apps offer high functionality in their free versions but nudge users to upgrade to avoid minor frustrations, such as advertisement breaks or limited content streaming controls.

We don't always recognize freemium business models at first glance

Although we typically think of freemium as being software that we, as consumers, may choose to pay for, it's also important to recognize that some of the biggest names in business remain, in many ways, freemium companies.

Most popular search engines and social media platforms can also be thought of as freemium services. The difference is that we're not paying for the product. We are the product.

Let's look at Google. As consumers, we think of Google as a free service. We ask questions, and Google points us in the direction of the answer. That's how we *use* it, but that's not how advertisers see it.

In theory, advertisers are featured in Google searches without having to lift a finger or pay a penny. Simply by virtue of having a website, its content gets picked up by the Google "crawlers" that index the website based on explicit keywords. The first few listings featured on most consumer searches on Google aren't those 'organic' listings, however. Companies who want to appear first have to outbid their website competitors in keyword auctions, the real money machine behind Google. Want to launch a new authentic African vegan mayonnaise as a startup entrepreneur? No problem. The Big Tech social media brands offer you their advertising platform. You just need to outcompete Unilever and P&G's marketing budget to claim the same keywords of interest that prevent you from getting any relevant exposure whatsoever.

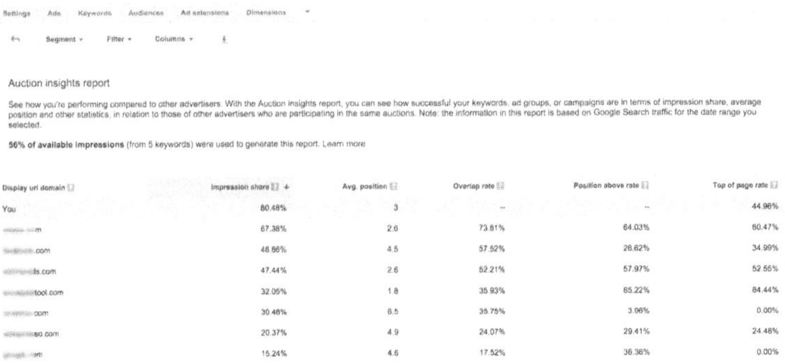

Settings Ads Keywords Audiences Ad extensions Dimensions

Segment Filter Columns

Auction insights report

See how you're performing compared to other advertisers. With the Auction insights report, you can see how successful your keywords, ad groups, or campaigns are in terms of impression share, average position and other statistics, in relation to those of other advertisers who are participating in the same auctions. Note: the information in this report is based on Google Search traffic for the date range you selected.

56% of available impressions (from 5 keywords) were used to generate this report. Learn more

Display url domain	Impression share	Avg. position	Overlap rate	Position above rate	Top of page rate
You	80.48%	3	--	--	44.96%
m	67.38%	2.6	73.81%	64.03%	60.47%
.com	48.86%	4.5	57.52%	26.62%	34.99%
ls.com	47.44%	2.6	62.21%	57.97%	52.56%
tool.com	32.05%	1.8	35.93%	85.22%	84.44%
com	30.48%	6.5	35.75%	3.96%	0.00%
so.com	20.37%	4.9	24.07%	29.41%	24.48%
m	15.24%	4.6	17.52%	36.36%	0.00%

Figure 10 - Popular search platforms offer advertisers "Auction Insights" which allow them to compare their campaigns with those of the competition and show them where they need to bid more to outcompete their competitors on relevant keyword search terms.

What does this mean for us?

If advertisers are Google's customers, we've become their merchandise. They are auctioning our profiles and attention to the highest bidder. There's nothing conceptually wrong with this since, often, that's exactly what we're looking for - instant gratification. But it's important that we're at least aware that our attention has become an auctionable product and our intimate behavioral profiles a valuable commodity.

The worry lies in how Google can improve what they offer to their customers. After all, not all attention is of equal value to a particular company. To improve their service, Google is offering advertisers more and more information about the people they're advertising to.

At some point, the level of information being offered to advertisers about us becomes so rich and intimate that it's no longer just our attention that's being sold. It's something more fundamental to our sense of self. And that's because it has become so incredibly easy for any wannabe entrepreneur to access these intimate profiles and start bidding on keywords to target any random product, service, or fake news propaganda to a hyper specific consumer niche that can be qualified based on the most intimate and granular levels of preference in hobbies, travel, sports, arts, school, music, games,... you name it. If it's ever typed in by someone on Google or Facebook, advertisers can *target* this 'persona' with any advertisement message provided it's free of pornography or hate speech.

This isn't to say that Google and Facebook are the enemy. Far from it. The relationship is, of necessity, at least somewhat symbiotic. These companies only have a product because we're willing to trade our attention for something we value; often information or social connection.

But we must appreciate that we're not their clients, and these organizations don't necessarily always have our best interests at heart. At the end of the day, they remain a for-profit business with a mission to make more money for their shareholders. The raw material that is being merchandised to make their money, is our intimate online behavior and resulting user profile on their platforms.

How much time are we spending on freemium services?

When we first started talking about freemium services, you may have considered skipping this chapter. If you don't play online games or pay for upgrades to free software, you might have assumed that freemium content just isn't a part of your life.

As we now see, social media and social networking sites are also a form of freemium, even though we're not being asked to pay for premium features. This might begin to make clear just how much of our lives are spent interacting with freemium products, and why it poses such a deep concern.

In 2021, the average adult spent 16 hours and 48 minutes per week on social media sites. For teenagers, it's just over 21 hours per week.

With social media use so high, even before we bring in any other freemium products, we're giving companies and advertisers huge opportunities to influence our thinking and our behavior, and our children are even more exposed than we are.

This begs the question, what's actually happening to us during this entertaining online time?

AI is reinforcing your prejudice

The short answer to what is happening to us when we spend so much time on social media is simple. Our social feeds are providing lip service. Even more of the same virtual comfort food, crying for your attention and sponsored by advertisers that are 'nudging' you to buy their product while they catch you off guard, indulging your favorite content during your relaxation time).

Social media giants are acutely aware that they are selling our attention. Their aim is to harvest as much of it as they can. In fact, they are so aware of the problem that comes with popular extremist propaganda that they are creating independent boards to assess whether a particular message or campaign can be ethically allowed or not in view of the potential societal impact. Popular product brands typically have dramatically more exposure than extremist propaganda, and yet only recently have such panels been suggested to query their social impact. What about the social impact of the popular product brand ads that don't particularly contribute to mental or physical well-being? Shouldn't those be reviewed by independent ethical boards too?

The first thing to understand about the use of AI in social media algorithms is that they're predominantly a numbers game. These algorithms don't 'recognize' or categorize content in the way we do. The AI doesn't work out that you love cats and then pick out all the videos with cats in them to show you it just looks like it does.

In fact, the algorithms use data from huge groups of people to find common trends. Remember the concept of "co-occurrence" to detect meaningful relations. It won't look at a video you liked and *understand* that it was a cute cat. It'll see that you liked that video and link you with thousands or millions of other people who took the same actions as you.

So, what does this mean? Well, this is how something goes viral. People with similar historical behavioral profiles get 'suggested' this content by the algorithm and, in most cases, will indeed behave as expected and interact with the recommended content. That strategy increases the number of people it will be shown to exponentially. It increases the likelihood of the content "going viral". If lots of them interact with it, it'll be seen even more. If people who like the content we like start interacting with different kinds of content, we'll start seeing more of that too. For newsworthy content, this is a powerful and useful tool. When designed to stalk you with unsolicited advertisements that feed your subconscious cravings, it's much more questionable.

It's also only looking at the times we've chosen to interact with a piece of media, by watching a video or posting a retweet, for example. Anything that we don't respond to is seen as a little bit less relevant, and that's really important.

Sometimes, this is something we welcome. If our Aunt Anne keeps sending out misinformation or annoying memes, we can just stop interacting with her, and we'll see less and less of what she posts. So far, so good.

The downside of this engagement-focused algorithm is that it will increase *anything* we interact with, whether it's a positive interaction or not. If someone posts something we deeply disagree with and we respond, guess what? We see more of that kind of content too and so do others who social media has determined 'like us'.

This means that the content we see on social media is skewed towards things that people feel passionately about, in both directions. Contentious, divisive, and polarizing content is king in an engagement-driven environment.

Those of us who've watched Bambi with our children have probably reminded them once or twice about Thumper's father's rule. "If you can't say something nice, don't say nothing at all." However much we might try to bring our children up in this way, social media is pushing the exact opposite message.

Outrage is marketing gold in the social media age

It's important to note that the manipulation within the social media freemium model isn't confined to the social media platforms themselves.

In an increasingly polarized world, companies are being expected to take a stand on social issues, and they're well aware that they're going to outrage whichever side they don't pick. You might have had some sympathy for companies in this position in the past. After all, they're just trying to do the right thing, and they're going to lose customers whichever way they go.

Well, maybe not.

Taking a public stand on contentious social issues often isn't the kind of business risk that it appears. We've seen that companies understand their customers intimately, sometimes better than we know ourselves. They can make a calculated decision as to which side of a social issue best fits their brand image and will lead to greater revenue.

Importantly, the resulting backlash is often the reaction they're hoping for.

Passing comment or taking a stand on important social issues regularly results in very public 'boycotts'. Boycotts in the past were private affairs. They simply require that you avoid purchasing from a particular company.

Today we see outraged customers creating video content of themselves destroying products from the company that has "betrayed" them. Many post videos of themselves burning their own Nike shoes, for example.

This highlights the deep truth behind the statement that "there's no such thing as bad publicity". This type of content may seem to present a problem for companies, but it's actually a huge opportunity. These boycotts often reach the national and international press. Levels of engagement on social media skyrocket, and loyalty amongst customers who support their position similarly explodes.

Importantly, these boycotts are also typically very short-lived and low impact. In fact, it seems that many of the people who destroyed their products actually purchased replacements. 'There's no such thing as bad publicity' appears to be an understatement in social media land.

So far, this might seem relatively benign. Companies are raising social issues, and are benefiting from doing the right thing. But when we think about this in the context of our previous discussion of the role of AI in polarizing social and political opinion, it can start to feel a great deal more uncomfortable.

Even when these campaigns are trying to achieve something for the social good, they are still contributing to the increasingly polarized world we live in. More importantly, they are benefiting directly from that polarization. And, whether intentionally or not, it's happening by stealth.

For example, Gillette's 'The Best a Man Can Get' campaign attempted to show a wider variety of behaviors as 'masculine' to oppose toxic masculinity and harmful masculine stereotypes such as "boys don't cry". Their adverts were trying to show boys that they could be empathic and kind, and still be masculine. Despite this laudable aim, their adverts generated intense controversy which led to influencers making videos, and their adverts even being aired (for free, obviously) on national news reports. A social good, but also good social marketing.

None of the time we spend paying attention to the latest controversy is included in evaluations of our exposure to marketing. We're so preoccupied with the social issue and trying to find a solution for our fractured social world that we overlook the marketing aspect of these campaigns. They are using those who disagree with them to capitalize on our emotions.

Well-intentioned or not, we need to think seriously about whether this is a degree of power we're happy to hand over.

The rise of 'influencers': How trust can go wrong

Social media has also led to the rise of 'influencers'. Put simply, these are people who have developed huge online followings and make their living from the advertising revenues associated with their posts. For the top influencers, this can be incredibly lucrative, but it often comes with a cost.

As I've said about other areas of freemium, there's nothing intrinsically wrong with this model. Content creators **should** receive some of the financial rewards from their efforts. It becomes an issue when those influencers put their own personal gain above the best interests of their followers.

Influencers build up a trust-based relationship with their followers. When they accept a lucrative marketing contract to promote particular products, they often don't feel the need to fully disclose this. As a result, the trust relationship can be (mis)used to promote a hidden agenda.

Think of it this way: When you go to a financial advisor for advice, you expect them to be making recommendations about what's best for you, not suggesting products with the biggest commissions. This is a legal requirement of being a fiduciary. There is very limited legal or social expectation placed on influencers, where there should be a lot more in view of the blind trust our children place in them.

Commercial 'nudging' is inevitable, and that's ok

We might not explicitly welcome manipulation within freemium products, but we have accepted it to some extent as an inevitable part of capitalism. And we need to at least be explicit about that.

It's a simple fact of life that we sometimes accept things that we deeply dislike in exchange for something that we value. For example, we will campaign for better streetlights, lower speed limits near schools, and safer crossings to try to keep our children safe from traffic. We wouldn't, however, support a national speed limit of 5 mph. Even though this would effectively eliminate road deaths, it would be extremely disruptive to our economy and way of life, and may even end up costing more lives in other ways (for example, by slowing response time for emergency services).

In a similar vein, removing all 'nudges' from advertising and marketing is both logically and practically impossible without the complete destruction of our capitalist model. In fact, it might not even be possible then.

'Nudging' isn't necessarily a bad thing. Many people like to be 'nudged' as a form of exploratory entertainment and discovery. Not many people, however, like to be 'manipulated' below conscious awareness. Manipulation is, in some ways, just a term for influence that we would rather someone else didn't have over us. And advertising is all about influence. We need to balance our response. Calling out malign manipulation is important, but we also don't want to overreact to legitimate, ethical interactions and influence.

The dangers of freemium: Addiction

Having said that some degree of manipulation is inevitable, we do need to talk about one example where we really can draw the line between influence and manipulation.

It would be a derogation of responsibility to discuss freemium content, especially in the context of its relationship to children's development, without talking about the relationship between freemium business models and addiction.

Numerous studies have taught us two important lessons about the nature and causes of addiction. Firstly, some individuals are predisposed to addiction issues. These are sometimes referred to as "addictive personalities", but however you wish to describe it, the fact remains that some people are just more likely to be subject to addiction. Twin studies have demonstrated that identical twins are more likely to display similar addiction behaviors than non-identical twins. In fact, twins who grew up apart as a result of adoption also have very similar patterns of addiction.

The second observation is that some situations make it much more likely that *any* individual will develop an addiction of some kind. Poverty, a lack of mental stimulation, and an absence of hope all lead to huge increases in addiction. Experiments in rats have shown that rats in enhanced living conditions ignore addictive drugs, whilst those in deprived conditions will use them extensively and suffer if they are removed.

But why is this relevant to freemium? Much freemium content, and freemium games in particular, is funded through competitiveness between users, and the desire to 'win'.

Freemium games with 'pay-to-win' models will typically include a significant random factor, with players receiving different rewards from identical purchases. This model is popular because it leads to far higher revenues than any other because users start to show addiction-based thinking and behaviors.

The 'sunk-cost fallacy' is a widespread example of such behavior. This phenomenon occurs when users are reluctant to abandon a strategy or course of action because they have invested heavily in it, even when abandonment would rationally be more beneficial. They are willing to spend more as long as they haven't yet obtained the reward they were hoping for. The money that they have spent is already considered lost, written off or 'sunk', increasing the hunger for redemption.

Addiction is also associated with 'all-or-nothing' thinking and several other cognitive biases. Once someone has developed these thought patterns, they are more susceptible to further addictions, even if they are in recovery from their original addiction.

The manipulations used to profit from freemium games *aimed primarily at children* are reinforcing thought patterns that can be linked to lifelong addiction issues, even if only in susceptible individuals. I would argue that this suggests that we need to think very hard about exactly how much manipulation is acceptable, and where we need to draw the line.

Can freemium services actually benefit humanity, or are we holding on to false hope?

So far, our dive into the world of freemium has looked particularly bleak. We see a slightly murky world where consumers have become products and manipulation is rife. Does this mean that freemium is somehow intrinsically bad or harmful?

I would like to argue that it doesn't. Although we can (and should) have deep concerns about some of the directions freemium content has taken, and the impact it has on our children, the model itself can be used to our benefit, and it often is.

Search engines are a great example of this. We, as consumers, are aware that our attention is the product these search engine companies sell to their clients who are willing to pay for exposure. In an instant, we are happy to give entrepreneurs the opportunity to advertise to us in exchange for access to the information we would like in an instant.

The relationship here really is symbiotic. We use search engines extensively because they provide us with something we value (easy access to accurate information). The world's leading search engine company manages advertisers to bid against each other for keywords *because* commerce is now virtually guaranteed thanks to its four billion worldwide users, even with a startup budget. They are motivated to keep improving their algorithms to prioritize informative websites and to understand our search queries in order to keep providing us with the instant gratification we've learned to expect.

Try to imagine a world in which search engines are no longer providing their consumer services for free. Imagine if you had to pay for every search you carried out. What would that mean? Would we get better quality service? I would argue we probably wouldn't. The most likely outcome would be that we would spend less time asking questions, be less inclined to look for evidence, and society itself would be less well-informed.

Not really the social change I think we're all hoping for.

Freemium services can, and do, provide a real service to society. There's tremendous value in connecting people and their exchange of information. But at the same time, some side effects can (and do) present real risks. The challenge for us is to fully understand the extent of the 'in kind' contracts we are engaging in and know how exactly our data is being used. After all, who really reads the dozens of pages of legal small print that we're semi-forced to accept if we want to continue using the freemium service we have grown to rely on?

Understanding how our data is being used, and potentially misused, is concerning for many readers. If you're one of them, I would recommend investigating a related initiative called 'Solid' from the inventor of the internet himself, Sir Tim Berners Lee. This initiative offers you the ability to control access to your personal data, to limit companies' ability to use it, and even to 'auction' it yourself, should you wish to.

Governments or society: Who is responsible for changing corporate behavior and who has the power?

It is helpful to look at what protections, both regulatory and societal, exist to encourage freemium companies to minimize manipulative behavior and to maximize the benefits for users.

The social pressures on social media companies have been increasing exponentially over the last few years, and this shows no signs of letting up. Importantly, those social pressures have started to be reflected in a push for government regulation.

Unfortunately, mere social pressure is unlikely to be sufficient to incentivize companies to take action to prevent our children from experiencing excessive or unwarranted exposure, especially when it is so lucrative. The current failures of major social media companies to address the consequences of their business decisions, either on our political narrative or on the mental health and body perception of our children, reinforces this impression.

Instead, we need governments to step in and set clear, legally-binding standards around how we expect companies to behave. This isn't about suggesting that all companies are bad, or that companies will only do the right thing if they are forced. It's about setting standards that protect our society.

Most of us are decent, kind people. We want to do the right thing. We wouldn't steal, even if we believed that we could do so without consequences. And yet we have laws against theft. Creating laws doesn't mean we're assuming that most people need to be told not to behave badly. It's a way of protecting us from those who are willing to cause us harm.

The same is true of government regulation. Creating regulations is a way that we, as a society, can place limits on what we consider acceptable behavior from corporations. If done correctly, creating these regulations doesn't actually stifle innovation and creativity. Rather, it increases it. When the old, harmful practices are no longer available, companies are forced to try new things and seek out new solutions. By regulating effectively, we create a need for innovation that companies are then keen to meet.

By regulating, we are also setting the parameters for that innovation. We are sending the message that companies will have to consider the physical, psychological, emotional, and social implications of their actions.

The solutions aren't easy, but they're coming

I have said from the start that regulation will be a key component of any solution to the risks posed to our children by our current advertising ecosystem. I have also been trying to highlight just how pervasive and invasive our media and marketing landscape has become.

By now, I trust that you have developed a keen sense of the scale of the task we have taken on. This isn't just about asking for minor changes, nor yet about demanding vast swathes of unchecked regulation.

This is a complex, nuanced, and genuinely vast problem, that will require deep thought, careful deliberation, and inspired innovation. Those same minds that develop freemium content will need to be part of the teams that brainstorm how we can mitigate its effects.

In the next phase of the book, we are going to look in greater detail at how we might go about creating solutions. Before we go there, I leave you to ponder one of the quotes from the popular Netflix documentary "The Social Dilemma":

"We've created a world in which online connection has become primary. Especially for younger generations. And yet, in that world, anytime two people connect, the only way it's financed is through a sneaky third person who's paying to manipulate those two people. So we've created an entire global generation of people who were raised within a context with the very meaning of communication, the very meaning of culture, is manipulation."

— Jaron Lainer, computer scientist and virtual reality pioneer

Chapter 6
Making capitalism work for us: How research bridges the gap between advertising and education

"Situations emerge in the process of creative destruction in which many firms may have to perish that nevertheless would be able to live on vigorously and usefully if they could weather a particular storm."

- Joseph A. Schumpeter

Chapter 6 Executive Summary:

- University spin-offs can challenge major tech firms more than grassroots community organizations who lack credible alternatives.
- If university spin-offs don't retain their independence long enough, their ability to

effect profound and lasting paradigm shifts is curtailed.
- Technology innovation is the greatest catalyst we have for driving positive change.
- There is a global need to improve the type of education that cultivates creativity and inclusive innovation.

Progress is a journey

In this chapter, we are going to look at how we might transition from where we currently are, where advertising reigns free, to a world where a well balanced education takes center stage.

From everything we've covered so far, it's clear that advertising (and the technologies behind it) represents a huge feature of our lives. We've come to consider advertising an unavoidable, natural, and often even entertaining part of western popular culture. Advertising has become so familiar to us that its omnipresence fits into our subconscious belief system as a prerequisite for sustainable progress and prosperity. The idea of Big Tech developing ever more clever ways of improving the advertising business doesn't strike us as necessarily detrimental. But we may need to pause and consider carefully which side-effects these new technologies may actually be scaling up in parallel.

University spin-offs: The grassroots antidote to Big Tech

One of the most powerful weapons we have in the attempt to defend ourselves against intrusive AdTech comes in the form of university spin-off companies. These typically occur when academics (often working with smaller companies) discover something which could potentially be made marketable as part of their studies. They typically partner with more experienced entrepreneurs and form dedicated companies that attempt to create an innovative commercial application.

University spin-offs occur in a wide variety of fields. Moderna, which created one of the major COVID vaccines, was originally a university spin-off.

The advantages of university spin-offs over more traditional start-up companies are significant. They are founded by people who have a deep understanding of their subject, and often have some form of societal good at the core of their mission.

Moreover, they are often based on much more fundamental research when compared to corporate R&D. Fundamental research brings the promise of truly disruptive innovation - the kind that challenges the status quo -, as opposed to incremental innovation - like the kind that increases your computer processing speed every 18 months.

In many ways, a university spin-off enters the business game halfway through. They already have their big idea, and a good amount of research to suggest that their aims are achievable. This enables them to skip the very earliest stages of research and development. Obviously, there will still be a great deal of work to be done, but a clear 'proof of concept' allows them to raise funds far more easily than it would be possible to finance the very earliest stages of R&D.

This is important because the Big Tech firms are well known for their disinclination to tolerate prospective challengers, no matter how weak they may seem at the time.

In this way, university spin-offs can often present more of a grassroots challenge to the major tech firms than actual grassroots community organizations. They combine expertise with purpose and are often run by people driven to see their ideas become reality. Of course, not all university spin-offs are successful, or indeed benevolent. But they represent the best chance we have of creating meaningful 'paradigm shift' change.

For university spin-offs, independence is everything

One of the biggest difficulties faced by university spin-off companies when it comes to creating change is the challenge of remaining genuinely independent.

As we have already explained, university spin-off companies often begin with the earliest stages of R&D already completed. Financing the transition from 'proof of concept' to a functioning product can be surprisingly tricky. Especially in the case of disruptive innovation. The company has to find substantial funding to tide them over the development gap until they can start generating a self sustaining revenue stream. And revenue only comes in once they have a compelling product or service that convinces early adopters.

This is where venture capital comes in, but this presents its own dangers. The Big Tech firms will regularly invest in smaller start-ups and university spin-offs, either directly or indirectly via affiliated Corporate Venture

Funds, VC's or Accelerators. It's not uncommon for the bigger firms to capitalize on these investments by either acquiring and shelving a potentially threatening technological development, or scaling and merging a strategic innovation so it blends in their bigger, more established solution.

If university spin-offs don't retain their independence long enough, their ability to effect profound and lasting 'paradigm shift' changes is often curtailed.

Angel investors are often suggested as an alternative investment source. Business 'angels' represent high net worth individuals who choose to fund smaller start-ups in exchange for a stake in the company. However, many of these high-net-worth individuals made their money in the big corporate establishment and often do not have deep enough pockets to cover the entire R&D funding gap on their own. Many of them have unrealistic expectations of quickly winning the startup lottery to compensate for their bet on the founder becoming the next Zuckerberg.

We need a shake-up of the way investment in start-up companies works if we are to realize the full benefits of university spin-offs. One option might be to encourage more pension funds and other, independent 'evergreen' funds to move into this area. Unfortunately, start-ups represent higher-risk investments than pension funds are typically willing to take. This may be a missed opportunity, as several pioneering examples demonstrate. A partnership between KU Leuven (Europe's top-ranking university for innovation) and local financial institutions created an evergreen seed fund that propelled the entire country's tech economy to the international top.

Innovation is the catalyst for positive change

Over the last several decades, we have seen many examples of the power of an idea whose time has come. Almost all of the biggest companies of our time were founded in the 1970s or later, and many of them are incredibly recent given their power and influence. These are global powerhouses and household names, such as Microsoft (1975), Apple (1976), Amazon (1994) Google (1998) and Tesla (2003).

Each of these huge corporations started out as an innovative idea, and each of them has contributed to enormous social change. Despite the legitimate concerns we may have around some of their business practices, there's no denying that these companies have changed the way we live and that many of those changes have been hugely positive.

Innovation is the greatest catalyst for driving positive change that we have, and the examples above highlight that this isn't just a hypothetical power. Again, we shouldn't be scared of trying to tackle the big problems. Enormous social change is happening all around us. Our role is to help facilitate innovation and direct that change to ensure that it serves us and protects our children.

Market research technologies are ripe for innovation, and a valuable stepping stone

When we've been talking about neuromarketing and market research technologies, we've been addressing them from the perspective of the corporations that typically make use of them. There is another story to tell, however.

A number of university spin-offs and research technology firms (including my own Mindspeller) are working hard to use these same tools in a transparent and empowering way; to increase our awareness of how data science is being used, and even to openly work to level the playing field for businesses of all different sizes.

In doing so, these firms are giving us our power back. They are helping us as consumers to improve our resistance to unwanted influence, and are encouraging us to question what forms of market research technology we're happy to allow into society and which we would rather place limits on.

As these companies grow and gain prominence, consumers will become more informed about the technologies being used, and their costs and benefits. This will also encourage more people to grapple with the questions and concerns we've been discussing throughout this book.

As we reach a more level playing field for a wider range of companies, and as consumers becoming more engaged with important questions of ethics and the welfare of our children, the move towards a role for companies in broadcasting educational material (which I'll elaborate on in the next few chapters) will begin to feel more achievable and powerful.

It's not just a stepping stone: Research technologies can stand on their own two feet

Our eventual goal is to deploy the marketing skill sets of large corporations (safely) towards our goal of educating our children smarter. Before we do that, however, I think it's important to clarify that market research technologies are hugely valuable in their own right.

We're not trying to replace or eliminate any part of our current advertising or marketing ecosystem. The solutions I'm suggesting are about shifting the balance of the market, prioritizing aspects of marketing that are currently firmly on the margins, and bringing in new ideas and innovations to better humanity.

Market research technology isn't the enemy, and neither is advertising technology nor corporations. This is a complex ecosystem that has grown and developed over nearly a century. We do need to change how this ecosystem works, but we still want it (and all its components) to thrive.

How do we know what we need?

If we want to look at the ways in which consumerism is able to serve our needs (and the ways in which it can't), it may be helpful to take a moment here to understand what our needs as consumers actually are.

One of the most well-known (and clearest) models for our needs as individuals is Maslow's hierarchy of needs. This combines several different important concepts.

Firstly, we have many different needs. Some of these are physical, while others are social, emotional, psychological, and even spiritual. In this context, therefore, we are thinking of a 'need' not as something required for basic survival, but as something we require if we are to be able to thrive.

It also acknowledges that we may not always be able to have all of our needs met. Some of our needs may be very difficult to meet. The important thing to remember is that we will continue to strive to have our needs met. In this respect, our needs can be seen less as specific requirements, and more as dominant drivers of our behavior. In consumer neuroscience, these needs are referred to as 'implicit goals'.

Finally, not all of our needs are equal. Hence, we have a hierarchy. Some needs will need to be fulfilled before we have the capacity to fulfill other needs that lie higher up Maslow's pyramid.

Beyond the basic: how do we address higher-order needs?

Probably the biggest achievement of consumerism and capitalism globally has been that we have been able to meet the most basic needs of the overwhelming majority of the population on a global scale. As technologies improve, many in the Western world have attempted to purchase their way to fulfilling their higher-order needs, such as self-esteem or respect. I suspect the most we can say is that they have had variable success with this strategy.

Throughout the rest of the world, however, basic needs have become far more achievable, although, as surging global inequality suggests, so have the most extravagant needs. Housing, shelter, food, and clean water have all become more easily available, and available in areas that might otherwise have struggled.

As basic needs are met, whether individually or globally, our motivation starts to move to higher-order needs. So, what's the next level of need on a global scale?

There are several potential candidates for the next big 'need' that could be addressed. There are concerns about global 'loneliness epidemics' (although these are more focused on the Western, materialistic world). Meeting the communication and basic IT needs of the world could have a huge impact. Both justice and social justice are needs that all of us would benefit from being met to a greater extent than they currently are[1]. And, of course, there are health needs, as has been highlighted by the global pandemic.

I'm not suggesting for one moment that any of those wouldn't be a valuable direction for our efforts, but I would like to suggest an alternative. There is a need across the world for more and better education (especially if more education can be achieved *without* more formal schooling). If we can find a way for consumerism to drive greater educational access and achievement on a global scale, we will see improvements in many of those other concerns as well.

Education is the silver bullet. The question is, can consumerism help us realize it?

Prompting businesses to meet educational needs: A complex task, but whose responsibility?

Is it possible for companies and advertisers to play a role in education safely? I believe it is, although with the very firm caveats that I'll detail later in this book. I also believe that this change can benefit both companies and society more generally.

If this is both possible, and carries advantages for all parties, it's reasonable to ask why these changes haven't already begun.

In fairness, I think it's safe to say that there are many fantastic ideas in all areas of life that are not currently being implemented because "that's just not the way we do it," but in this case, I think there may be something more to it.

Moving into a more educationally-based model might be great for companies in the long run, and it's certainly an advantage for society right from the start, but it's almost certainly going to be associated with a significant degree of uncertainty and upheaval in the short and medium-term. Companies are understandably reluctant to take on those risks (even for a potential benefit) *when other companies are not going to do the same.*

Corporations are, by their 'for-profit' driven nature, very much like herd animals. Staying close to others and mimicking behavior both increase (financial) security. If you start to do something wildly out of the ordinary, you risk losing investors, your profits can fall, and your position becomes vulnerable.

This is why we are going to talk in later chapters about the importance of regulation, and the role the government will need to play in helping to bring about change. Because staying with the herd makes sense when things are settled. When everything is unsettled and no one's quite sure which way to jump, then we can expect to see courageous leadership and exciting developments.

Chapter 7
Democratizing Consumer Neuroscience

"We cannot let commercialization of education come in the way of democratization of education."

— Sharad Vivek Sagar

Chapter 7 Executive Summary:

- Knowing *that* we are being manipulated by advertising can be a first step in limiting the influence.
- Educated consumers are more immune to manipulation, materialism and mental disease.
- Helping bring about change requires the freedom to think critically about mainstream

cultural biases and the world we currently live in.

- Whistleblowers can help improve child mental well-being by challenging the status quo in the advertising sector, a charitable cause worthwhile mobilizing your community.

We are not helpless consumers

At this point, I think it's important to reiterate one of the fundamental points I made back in Chapter 1. This situation is urgent, but it is absolutely not hopeless.

Much of the conversation around the topics of consumer neuroscience and the ethics of capitalism portrays us as helpless consumers, unable to take action or influence the decisions of global corporations. I think that's a profoundly disempowering way to think about the economic structures we live within.

Yes, there is a great deal of power in the neuromarketing tools companies have been deploying. Yes, there is a huge capacity for us to be 'nudged' and maneuvered into taking actions that are not necessarily in our best interests. But we also have the ability to step back from the information that is being presented to us, to ask questions, and (importantly) to find answers.

More than ever before, knowledge is power.

In some cases, simply knowing that we are being manipulated is enough to remove the influence. As parents of young children, you've probably heard the phrase "but Mom/Dad lets me do it!" As a manipulation, this fails at least partly because it's so utterly transparent.

There are other examples where this really isn't the case, but being aware of the manipulations around us does still mitigate the effects significantly. For example, young people are exposed daily to social media images of influencers and even their peers, which have been subjected to filters and other modifications to make them look perfect. Young women, in particular, are acutely aware of the impact of these filters, and they use them themselves to fulfill their implicit goals. While this awareness might not be enough to overcome the damage to their self-esteem (being subjected to a constant influx of vanity fairs), it helps limit the harm they might otherwise experience.

The more scientifically literate our population becomes, and the better they understand the power of the neuroscience behind many of these marketing and advertising decisions, the easier it will be to eliminate unethical and inappropriate practices, and the better protected we will be against the pressures that remain.

Giving information to consumers helps to level the playing field

Giving more information to consumers helps to level the playing field, not just between consumers and large corporations, but also between huge, multinational conglomerates and small start-ups.

One of the difficulties for smaller companies trying to compete with major corporations is that they simply can't afford the same levels of marketing research, advertising, sponsorship, and general reach that the larger organizations have at their disposal. Even without larger corporations actively attempting to retain their top spot by outcompeting smaller competitors, the playing field simply isn't level.

As consumers become more aware of the techniques in use and as transparency around advertising increases, consumers will be able to recognize companies that are trying to unduly influence us and purchase our loyalty. This typically won't be enough to actually create a level playing field, but it may go some way towards reducing the very steep slope we're currently witnessing.

This is already happening to some degree, as more ethical consumers are trying to move away from companies that are known to treat their workers badly. These movements are not having an enormous impact yet, but they are gathering pace. The expedited adoption of ESG[1] reporting standards seems particularly promising.

Savvy consumers have started to use some of the techniques we have been discussing against these large companies to increase social pressure. Many students are still Amazon devotees, for example, but others view the distinctive packaging as a sign that the purchaser doesn't care about social issues or workers' rights. This creates a sense of stigma or shame, particularly on more progressive campuses, or students feeling the need to justify a purchase as necessary. Using social pressure and emotion to drive behavior change doesn't have to be the preserve of big companies. The more consumers understand the tools in use, the better equipped they will be to use similar tools themselves.

Importance of free will: Too much manipulation can begin to overwhelm our sense of self

At this point, it seems important to revisit the ideas around free will we discussed in Chapter 4. As I mentioned, one of the biggest threats to our free will wasn't that our actions were constrained or that there were consequences to our choices. The problem that I identified was that we are insufficiently aware of the countless 'nudges' and peer pressures that we are subjected to.

If we are unaware of the influence they can exert, companies could potentially put us in a position where our free will is substantially reduced. Improved information, communication, and understanding are the obvious antidotes to being unaware of what is being done to us.

As consumers become more aware of the tools and techniques being used, the threat to our free will is dramatically reduced.

I'd like to come back, for a moment, to Kastrup's whirlpool metaphor. We've been talking about free will without really referencing the state of the art in consciousness research introduced in Chapter 2, or thinking about what it would mean. One way to imagine a reduction in our free will would be that an external influence or 'ripple' (in this case, the advertising we were presented with) succeeds in 'disrupting' our whirlpool and making it unstable and vulnerable (perhaps to the extent of spinning out of control). This will then also have an impact on the ripples we, ourselves send out as well. If we're not in control of ourselves, it's virtually impossible to connect with others on a deeper level.

As adults, our whirlpool is robust enough to retain its form after the disturbances or pressures have passed, but what about children? Their sense of self, as distinct from others, is only just developing. Their understanding of who they are is in constant flux. They are still learning about what it means to have free will. Should we really allow advertising to interfere and complicate this already sensitive learning process?

Change comes from harnessing the dual powers of free will and motivation

I'm aware that talking about the idea of free will in the context of advertising and marketing can appear more than a little hyperbolic or over-dramatic, but we do need to take these kinds of questions seriously. If for no other reason than the understanding that creating change of any kind requires free will; freedom of thought and freedom of action are both essential for anyone trying to create change in any sphere of their life.

Creating change means having the freedom to think differently about the world we live in. We need to be able to imagine a world vastly different from the one we are experiencing. We need space to daydream, to imagine, and to mentally explore all of our different options.

We also need the freedom to act. This doesn't just mean that we are free from physical constraints. Given that I'm asking you to join me in our efforts to produce political and social change, it's only fair to be honest about the fact that it's going to cost us something, even if it's just the time it takes to further inform yourself. Those most passionate about the cause may want to devote time and energy to expediting change, and any parent in the modern world will tell you that they're not exactly over-endowed with either of those two resources. Personally, I walked away from a comfortable career in venture capital to test my entrepreneurial drive and pursue my vision. I'm not expecting others to do the same, and I want to recognize that each of us will have different constraints on our ability to push for social change.

Being aware of our constraints allows us to focus our efforts on the areas where we will be able to make the biggest difference.

If we have the freedom to think and the freedom to act, the final component to creating change is having the motivation to push, even when it's a challenge. So, where does your motivation come from?

Where is your motivation for creating change? Protecting your family and yourself?

For most of the people reading this book, I would argue that your motivation for wanting to change the world of advertising and marketing is to protect yourselves and your children. You have seen that there is a significant problem in the way these industries are currently working, and you are concerned that current business practices are doing them harm.

I hope that the information I've presented in this book so far has helped to confirm this perception. You're not wrong. There are practices out there that are damaging mental well-being, and this is absolutely a good reason to push for change.

Protecting the people you care about can be a powerful motivator, especially when you can see the risks and a solution is in sight. Unfortunately, it can also put you in a difficult position. Often, it inclines you to worry and become hyper vigilant rather than take action. Constant concern can be exhausting, and can therefore reduce your capacity for making change.

Seeing our children being influenced or adopting fake news is a powerful motivator for change

This kind of motivation can also start to wane as our children become older (although it may well re-emerge with a vengeance once grandchildren are on the horizon). As we worry less about our own children, the risks become impersonal and distant once more. But the real risk is the impact of an increasingly materialistic world on society as a whole. Youngsters' craving to "be a billionaire so bad" that their songs about it top the pop charts should question our cultural priorities.

We do not all need to see our children as unhappy, dysfunctional young people to be worried about society as a whole. We don't all need to see 'damage' first before we feel motivated to call for change. We all see our children doing their best in an imperfect world. And honestly, we're right to do so. I can't imagine how heartbreaking and challenging it would be to parent a child that's been deeply damaged by the world we helped to build.

We need to be just as motivated by thinking about maximizing their future opportunities

However, there is another way to think about how the world we live in is affecting our children. It's one that I personally find much more compelling.

Although we've been talking so far about the impact that advertising and marketing are having on our children, I like to think this same impact can also be used for good. Knowing more about the mechanisms used to 'nudge' consumers has been a powerful motivator for me to work towards ideas that have the potential to change the system.

We've explained that, when children are exposed to large amounts of ad sponsored, popular media content from a young age, they develop in subtly different ways. Their emotional reactions are skewed as a result of the constant pull of emotional advertising. Some will put up emotional walls, responding to all emotional stimuli as manipulative at a subconscious level. Others will have failed to create barriers to other people's emotions, based on an expectation that the world is full of emotions that they are meant to process. Whichever way they react, they have lost the opportunity to develop their own sense of emotional stability, and the kinds of relationships they could have built had they done so.

Our children can be perfect in our eyes, and they may have coped well with the media environment they were born into, but that doesn't mean that we don't want to make the world even better for them. Changing the media landscape to promote healthier development and an improved quality of life seems like an obvious step to me.

One way to think about our children's lost opportunities is to link them back to Kastrup's whirlpool metaphor. Our whirlpools represent our sense of ourselves as discrete and unique individuals. As we have already mentioned, for children, these whirlpools are unstable and in flux. One of the ways they learn about themselves as discrete individuals is by interacting with the ripples given off by other people and aspects of the world around us.

As a result of the high tech currently available in the world around us, children will be gaining advantages of ripples that we never experienced, but they may be missing out on some of the lower tech ones that really resonate and might help them reconnect with their natural intelligence.

Seeking out knowledge is the first (necessary) step towards creating change

Simply by reading this book as far as you already have, you are in a more powerful position to effect social, political, and economic change than you were before. The power that you have gained from your understanding is something that you can now spread to the people around you.

If we're trying to create an enormous ripple, we need to spread the word to as many people as we can. Hopefully, you're now a part of that mission. In such an interconnected world, we can each touch hundreds of "whirlpools", and create thousands of tiny ripples. In synchrony, these tiny ripples can turn the tide.

Most importantly, with the knowledge you now have, you are able to understand more about the ways that advertising firms are trying to understand, categorize, and condition you below conscious awareness. You are now able to use that knowledge to protect yourself and your friends and family. Even small things, like switching off the radio during the commercial break, can prevent unsolicited priming.

You are already a part of the solution.

Chapter 8
Corporate soul mates and Brand Equity

"Happiness is a psychological construct, the meaning of which everybody knows but the definition of which nobody can give."

- H. M. Jones cited in Lyubomirsky 2001

Chapter 8 Executive Summary:

- The pleasure we gain from something novel often only lasts as long as we see that item as new. This serves to highlight one of the dangers of linking happiness to consumerism.
- Due to the increased amount of advertising our children are exposed to, we can't extrapolate

from our own experiences with advertising and hope that everything will turn out ok for future generations.

- By desensitizing children and making advertising stand out again, we're allowing them to process the information mindfully, and teaching them the reflexes they will need to protect themselves for the rest of their lives.
- Investing in education opens up possibilities for leading happy lives that go beyond the traditional materialist paradigm.

Why we don't currently have a level playing field for consumer attention

When we think of a capitalist system (and when we explain it to our children), we tend to talk about how it is supposed to work. We explain that companies come up with products, and customers make rational choices based on which product is best for them. If another company produces a product that is objectively better, that company will grow, and the one offering an inferior product will start to fail.

This explanation presupposes a level playing field, however. In our current marketplace, that level playing field is nowhere in sight.

Firstly, we have a highly saturated market. It might not be saturated for any one product, but there are so many products available (and so many being thrust at us all day long) that we, as consumers, often don't have the time or energy to investigate every single product.

Secondly, we have a (relatively) small number of giant corporations who are able to wield disproportionate power, particularly when it comes to our attention. We've already discussed that the average person sees up to 10,000 pieces of advertising per day (and possibly more if we include 'hidden' advertising from social media influencers or the forms of 'outrage marketing' we talked about in Chapter 5). How many of those are likely to have come from small businesses? How many are from a local trader? And how many from a huge, multinational corporation?

When we think about products 'off the top of our head', almost all of them are based on subconscious priming, associations, and recall. It's only once we have narrowed our list down to a shortlist of a few 'familiar' brands (without really being consciously aware of it) that our rational mind starts to kick in to justify our purchase.

We never see the overwhelming majority of the products available to us, let alone take the time to find out whether they are a better fit for our needs. The idea of rational consumers making decisions based on the relationship between quality and price is a helpful fiction to explain economics to our children, but it is definitely still fiction.

What are the benefits to us as consumers of a more equitable situation between companies?

From what I've been saying above, it's hopefully clear that a dramatically uneven playing field for consumer attention isn't actually in the consumers' best interests or that of society in general.

When the system makes it difficult for smaller companies to gain a foothold, we're artificially reducing the amount of innovation in our society. You might have experienced the frustration of knowing exactly the kind of product you would like to purchase but not being able to find it. It probably won't make you feel better to know that there's most likely someone out there who has created that product and feels the exact mirror image of your frustration, their brand not finding its way to you. They know that you're out there wanting their product, but they just can't outcompete the bigger brands' advertising budgets. They end up in the long tail of a search result or social media feed where you don't find them.

A more equitable landscape would also typically mean a closer relationship between the quality of products and their price. A more level playing field would, by its very nature, require that consumers have more choices to help them make more informed decisions. Consumer demand would be more effective in driving innovation and product design.

I would like to highlight, however, that I've chosen my words very carefully here. I'm looking for a *more* level playing field. I want to *reduce* the power differential between smaller start-ups and global multinationals, not eliminate it. This isn't a form of hidden socialism. It's about evolving into a sustainable, thriving economy , and that requires genuine choice and viable competition to ensure that innovative young companies can flourish.

Where does consumerism go now? A choice between happiness or overconsumption

The most common metric used to understand and evaluate how well a country (or an economy) is performing is gross domestic product (GDP). This is the total value of all of the goods and services a particular country has produced during a specific time period (typically 1 year).

GDP is used to measure the growth of an economy year-on-year, and we use it as a more general measure of how well we're doing. The trouble is, GDP is much better at measuring our economy than it is at assessing our quality of life.

Until recently, GDP and quality of life were thought to be relatively closely linked. As we became more wealthy, we were able to buy more labor-saving equipment and enjoy more expensive and exotic luxuries.

More recently, however, researchers and the population in general have started to realize the truth in the old adage: "Money can't buy happiness."

This isn't to deny the existence of extreme poverty, nor to downplay the genuine horror that it leads to. However, the countries with the highest scores for happiness and wellbeing don't tend to be at the top of their class when it comes to GDP and growth either.

As a society, we are going to have to make a decision when it comes to the future direction of consumerism when it comes to: Do we focus on ever-increasing quantities of consumption, or are we aiming to focus on finding the best products that bring joy and happiness into our lives?

It's clear to me that overconsumption at the scale we are currently operating at simply isn't sustainable, either from an economic or an environmental perspective.

Law of diminishing returns

You may be familiar with the Law of Diminishing Returns. It's a concept that is applied in a wide variety of different contexts and in different ways. You might also know a variation of it as the 80/20 rule.

The law of diminishing returns suggests that we will typically get huge rewards for very little effort when we start a new activity. As we progress, we will find that our rewards become smaller, and the amount of effort we have to put in becomes significantly greater.

In the case of the 80/20 rule, the idea is that you can often achieve 80% of a task with about 20% of your total effort. The final 20%, however, will require 80% of your effort.

One of the places where the law of diminishing returns applies very strongly is in the brain. From a neuroscience perspective, our brains respond most strongly to new and novel stimuli. As something becomes commonplace, our neurons respond less and less.

If we take the example of eating a banana, assuming you like bananas, eating one will activate the pleasure centers of your brain. After eating several bananas, that activity diminishes and you develop something known as "sensory-specific satiety", which is an academic way of saying that you're getting a bit sick of bananas now.

If someone handed you an apple, on the other hand, the pleasure centers of your brain might well light up again.

This serves to highlight one of the dangers of linking happiness to overconsumption. Simply put, the pleasure we gain from something novel often only lasts as long as we see that item as new.

We've already addressed the dangers of rampant consumerism and observed that overconsumption simply cannot continue to grow exponentially without risking a tipping point when feelings of inequality escalate into social upheaval. The outdated neo-liberal models companies still use to drive our consumption are going to have to shift from questionable expectations of growth to models that promote sustainability, quality, and long term customer wellbeing over unbounded greed.

Brand loyalty in children: Should we be worried?

But what happens when we start to build brand loyalty among children. As we have pointed out repeatedly throughout this book, children process information from an emotional, rather than an intellectual, perspective. They aren't forming their brand loyalty on the basis of the quality of the products, the price relative to their budget, or the ethics and values of the brand. They're basing their loyalty on the subconscious appeal of the advertisement, and on their desire to fit in with their peers.

More than this, they are forming attachments that will shape their expectations for much of their adult lives.

We know that children absorb their understanding of what is 'normal' and 'right' during their early years and that this understanding is very robust. Even children in abusive households see their upbringing as normal. Much of psychotherapy and counseling involves helping adults to recognize and address damaging impressions of interpersonal relationships and how they should treat others and be treated in return.

The same is true of the values they adopt around brands and products. The kind of brand loyalty built during childhood is intense and unquestionable, and can easily create a kind of tribal allegiance. This comes with additional cognitive biases, meaning that they will overlook problems with their 'ingroup' brands and be heavily critical of non-favored options. It's important to remember at this point that influencers, including journalists, celebrities, and politicians, should be considered brands in and of themselves. They are, after all, making a living off of their (brand) name. The content they bring represents their product. Frequent and lopsided exposure to these types of 'influencer' brands during childhood arguably represents the most worrisome of all.

Any form of excessive brand loyalty isn't healthy for our children, especially as they move towards adulthood. Children are exposed to dramatically more direct and indirect advertising than we were at their age. We can't simply extrapolate from our own experiences and hope that everything will turn out ok in the end.

It's also not always a healthy position for companies and advertisers to be in. Excessive loyalty can easily drive complacency, where companies take their customers for granted and focus more on avoiding competition than they do on improving their products or services. This reduces innovation across the board, which hurts us all.

Reducing advertising to children avoids desensitization

Reducing children's exposure to advertising allows us to avoid them becoming fully desensitized to the level of manipulation and excess around us.

We've already talked about the way our brains highlight things that are novel, different, or changing. Things that are commonplace in our environment can become 'invisible'. This is why people living under the flight path of an airport stop noticing the noise, and why we don't see our own clutter at home but notice everything when we go to visit a friend.

This is the same process as when children (or adults) become desensitized to advertisements. Right back at the beginning of this book, we talked about the amount of advertising we see every day, and how difficult it can be for us to reconcile this with how much advertising we notice.

This effect is even greater if we have grown up with something. We've already discussed how the environment we grow up in has a huge influence on what we see as 'normal' or 'right'. When we limit the amount of advertising a child is exposed to, we are lowering their threshold for how much advertising is normal. We teach their brains that this new stimulus, crying out for attention, is something out of the ordinary.

This will lead them to devote more attention to advertising, which might sound like the exact opposite of our intentions, but it's actually an important step. Brainwashing happens when we're not paying attention to the messages we are being given. By making advertising stand out, we're allowing them to process the information mindfully, and teaching them the reflexes they will need to protect themselves for the rest of their lives.

Solutions will need to meet the needs of society, as well as protect our children

In writing this book, I've tried to focus very clearly on what I see as the biggest danger in our current media landscape; the impact on our children's development. As we move towards finding solutions, however, it's going to be important that we consider the full ecosystem around consumerism, marketing, advertising, and even product development.

The solutions that we offer need to be carefully tailored to ensure that all of these needs are still met. Without this awareness and careful planning, our efforts will fall at the first hurdle. If we can successfully integrate our understanding of the complex network of interconnected needs, however, success will be very much within our grasp.

In the following chapters, we will turn to my ideas on how to turn the tide, focusing on innovating education as the key catalyst. Research shows that the relationship between education and happiness is substantially different from the relationship between income and happiness. While there is evidence that higher income does not go hand in hand with higher happiness after a certain point, there is no evidence of a similar levelling-off in the relationship between education and happiness.

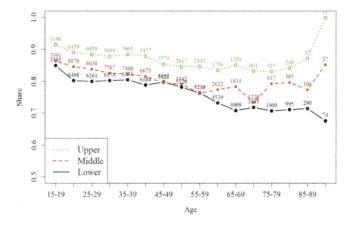

Figure 11 - Higher share of happy people amongst the educated. Source: Too Educated to be Happy? An investigation into the relationship between education and subjective well-being Erich Striessnig

The research paper by Erich Striessnig, cited above, concludes as follows:

"While there is evidence that higher income does not go hand in hand with higher happiness after a certain point, there is no evidence of a similar parabolic relationship between education and happiness. According to the information provided by the European and World Values Survey, that is far more comprehensive than any comparable data source, starting from any level of educational attainment, higher levels of education are related to – on average – higher probability of being happy. Thus, the educational system not only "channels people into two different life cycle tracks characterized by higher and lower income trajectories", as claimed by Richard Easterlin (2001, p.481). Education also seems to open up possibilities for leading happy lives that go beyond extending the consumption-possibility frontier."

"While better educated future generations can be expected to live healthier lives and to confront the big challenges of the 21st century more effectively without suffering in their well-being, there is also a risk that the increasing permeation of technology in our societies and the growing complexity will increase the divide between a well educated global elite and a vulnerable underclass characterized by low levels of education. This would bring us closer again to "the good life" envisioned by the ancient Greeks which was reserved mainly for the elites who were free to dedicate themselves to their education as others were doing the physical labor for them. While even in our days not everybody has a priori equal chances of living a happy life, chances have never been greater to make this project universal. Access to the educational system remains one of the most important factors to prevent avoidable unhappiness and to promote happiness."

Chapter 9
the ultimate teasers - Education on autopilot

"In the economy of action, effort is a cost, and the acquisition of skill is driven by the balance of benefits and costs. Laziness is built deep into our nature."

— Daniel Kahneman

Chapter 9 Executive Summary:

- While generally accepted as a crucial form of life insurance for our children and their future prosperity, the education system remains structurally underfunded.
- Billions of dollars are wasted every year on marketing experimentation worldwide, funds that could be used by advertisers to help

innovate the education system with formats that support their increasing need for ESG compliance.
- Encouraging companies to find ways to provide education around their area of expertise both reinforces their position as an authority on the topic and provides children with an education that is more exciting and relevant.
- Regulators can create environments conducive for companies to collaborate on producing high quality, peer reviewed educational content that exemplifies social responsibility.

Making change is hard: Aim for evolution, not revolution

Throughout the book so far, I've been talking about the scale of the changes needed, and have been describing some of the adjustments as being genuinely radical. And it's true. We are looking at a problem with enormous scope, and a world in which we have solved it will look dramatically different from the one we currently live in.

I've been trying to balance this reality with the (equally genuine) need to ensure that the changes we seek are realistic and achievable. That's not an easy circle to square.

The answer to this comes in the form of evolution, not revolution.

Revolutions are inherently destructive. They might be aiming for utopia, but revolutionaries are willing to break with our current world to get there. My take on that is simple. This is our world. My children live in it. I don't want to promote the kind of social upheaval that rushing or dramatic change requires.

Instead, I'm advocating a path of evolution. If evolution in nature can create everything from a jellyfish to a duck-billed platypus, I'm willing to believe that we can create incremental change to bring us to a healthier and more sustainable approach to advertising; one that supports our economy and *improves* the wellbeing of our children.

Was there ever enough funding in our school system?

If we're looking for solutions to the problem of our children being programmed or brainwashed by the sheer volume and sophistication of advertising in their environment, our first step has to be to look at the school system. We need to focus on their education. Empower them with the knowledge required to make them less susceptible to mental disease.

School should be a place where children are free from direct or indirect advertising. Even an attractive in kind sponsorship from a popular IT multinational, donating laptops or branded software to a local elementary school, should be carefully considered in view of the disproportionate brand familiarity such in kind sponsorship deals imprint on our children's minds from a very young age. That doesn't mean such a sponsorship deal cannot be accepted, but it does require due scrutiny and awareness of the fact that well framed brand exposure and experiential familiarization during childhood provide the brand with tremendous competitive advantages that last a lifetime. It's one of the most clever ways of beating the competition simply because of the sheer frequency of being exposed to the brand, and especially given the susceptible state of the brains of children under the age of 12. This is why Lego, Disney, and Barbie are some of the most valuable brands worldwide. You subconsciously prefer your children to experience these brands you have subconsciously learned to favor during your own childhood. For these hallmark brands, it's the gift that keeps on giving.

The school day is a significant period of time every day where children are interacting with their peers, learning to work with adults, learning social skills as well as subject-specific material. Hopefully, somewhere in amongst all of that, they also get to enjoy themselves; discover their artistic side, learn an instrument, try some poetry or join a sports team. The creative arts, humanities and social sciences require at least as much attention as the exact sciences, preferably more. Our intuitive, metaphoric minds have long been culturally stigmatized ever since Freud turned them into something dirty.

Given the world that they are being prepared for, we also need to expect (and even require) that schools offer children support and education around media literacy and online safety. These will be essential lessons that they will use daily for the rest of their lives.

One of the problems with this list of things children need from schools is that the school system almost never has the money it needs to be able to provide all of this at even the most basic level, let alone to the standards we have come to expect in the for-profit sector.

If we can demonstrate that advertising is creating, or at least amplifying, the need for educational initiatives around media literacy and online safety (and we can), it doesn't seem unreasonable to suggest that major corporations could contribute some of the funding needed. We expect polluters to help clean up our environment. Why shouldn't advertisers help provide our children with the protection they need to stay in good mental shape?

Associate branding with social good

We've discussed earlier how firms have started using social issues as an important part of their branding, and how this has sometimes led to an increase in polarization. Some companies have used divisive social issues to court controversy and increase their media presence. However, that doesn't mean that large corporations don't have an important role to play in tackling big social issues.

The main problem with the way that companies have been interacting with social issues has been that almost all of the attention paid to their efforts has been on contentious or polarizing issues. That's hardly surprising. We live in an incredibly polarized political and social climate, meaning that the list of uncontroversial social concerns is dwindling fast, and companies doing good without backlash simply isn't front-page news. As we've already discussed, social media engagement algorithms are unlikely to amplify those kinds of messages.

In an ideal media landscape, companies taking action to benefit society would receive plenty of attention, and create a feel-good factor for their brand that encourages others to do the same.

Educating our children should be an unequivocal social good, with no backlash. Obviously, there are some areas of education where that, sadly, isn't the case, and these would need to be handled carefully. But what if companies' normal advertisements were replaced by educational content that used the techniques currently used to build brand awareness but repurposed to reinforce learning.

When it comes to teaching math, languages, or history, for example, few people would object to companies exposing our children to entertaining, high-quality 'lessons' outside of the normal school day, provided those lessons didn't contain hidden marketing and were subjected to academic peer review.

Companies would be able to demonstrate their commitment to social responsibility, and our children would receive a better education. Importantly, we would come to associate our purchasing decisions with our understanding of how far a company is contributing to society.

Social expectations of corporate responsibility can change behavior

You would be forgiven for thinking that companies are simply too powerful to have their decisions influenced by us, as consumers, holding them to a higher standard. It can sound hopelessly idealistic, but I believe that it can have an astonishing impact.

I've already said that I'm an optimist by nature, but I'm not basing my belief on hope and optimism alone. We actually have evidence that social expectations around corporate behavior can drive that behavior.

In some parts of the world, there is a strong social expectation that companies will take advantage of every (legal) loophole to pay as little tax as possible. Indeed, this is often viewed as a responsibility they owe to their shareholders and "just common sense". But this expectation isn't the case everywhere.

In much of Scandinavia, people have very different expectations of the companies they interact with. They expect companies to pay the taxes they should, and this expectation is generally fulfilled. Lego, the Danish-based company, pays an effective tax rate of around 22%. This is a remarkably close match with Denmark's corporate tax rate of 22%. If you compare this with the United States, you'll see a headline tax amount of 21%, but many major corporations paying less than 4% effective tax rates over many years.

Obviously, there are many reasons for differences in tax paid by companies in different countries, but the social expectations aspect shouldn't be ignored. After all, shareholders and C-suite executives are themselves part of society and both absorb and reflect our values.

Companies have their own areas of expertise

The benefit of having companies engaged in our education system isn't just that they can provide funding. They have a lot more to offer than that.

Companies don't just make money. They're there to provide a product or service. And, behind that product or service, there's almost always something of important educational value. Encouraging companies to find ways to provide education around their area of expertise both reinforces their position as an authority on the topic and provides children with an education that is exciting and relevant.

No child left behind: How companies can provide important outreach

One of the biggest challenges teachers face today is the problem of children who feel distant and disengaged from their education. It's all too easy to dismiss them as "difficult" or "problem children," but we can (and should) do a lot more to include and engage them.

This absolutely isn't me jumping on the 'teachers aren't doing enough' bandwagon. With class sizes rising and the profound and long-term underfunding of our classrooms, I think it's unrealistic to expect teachers to catch every child.

Many children become disengaged because our current education system just doesn't seem relevant to them or their lives. For example, children have been complaining for generations that learning their times tables is pointless. Children today carry more processing capacity than powered the first moon landing in their pockets. It's hard to deny that they might have a point.

Including companies as one strand of the educational system helps young people to understand how their education will be relevant and keeps it grounded in the reality of their future working lives.

A preparation for work, or something more? The true purpose of education

If we are thinking of allowing companies to find a place in our education system, it is worth taking a few moments to think about the actual purpose of education. We understand that we need to send our children to school so that they can learn to read and write, but there's actually a little more to it than that.

For some people, the purpose of education is to prepare children for the world of work. We are training the workers of the future, and we need to give them the skills that their future employers will need them to have. This is why STEM[1] has become so popular.

If we follow this view of education, it's absolutely appropriate for companies to pay towards education. After all, we are spending huge amounts of taxpayers' money to train their future workers.

I would argue that this is a particularly bleak and limiting way of thinking about education. If this is the sole (or even the main) purpose of education, why would we offer music, dance, or art? Unless a child has the talent to make a career as a musician, dancer, or artist, these skills are unlikely to be of immediate, direct value to their eventual employer. Given my plea for a well-rounded curriculum, this criticism leads me to look for a different understanding of education rather than call for the creative arts to be removed from the curriculum.

If education is, as I have suggested, more than simply a long period of vocational training, what alternative purpose could it serve? A subtly different interpretation could be that our education system exists to help children learn the basics for multidisciplinary collaboration and discovery of their true passions, allowing them to seek out their future careers.

This way of thinking about the purpose of education offers a slightly more nuanced (and palatable) understanding and does at least allow for the idea that children should be experimenting and learning about all the different skills they might have. It still feels remarkably narrow, and mechanistic, however. After all, we require that children spend almost all of their first two decades in compulsory education. Surely it must aim to achieve something more than an extended careers day and occupational training?

For me, the answer again comes from our understanding of the philosophy of consciousness. Education is the process by which our children are able to control their whirlpool minds and prevent them from spinning out of control when confronted with external ripples they pick up on (eg. when interacting with children pursuing other disciplines). The more they are able to control their minds, the calmer their whirlpools become and the more in sync they become with the natural intelligence we all share.

Education, and becoming more in sync with our collective (sub)consciousness, will change *the nature* of the ripples children send out into the world. Learning about STEM might help them offer more to an employer, while the humanities and social sciences can help them to be more understanding as friends. Geography and biology can inspire them to see the world and bring back new ideas to inspire those around them. History and psychology allows them to see patterns and to understand that there is nothing inevitable about the way our world currently is.

This is dramatically wider in scope than the first possible purpose I described, but it also feels so very much more hopeful. We're not training our children to be cogs in a machine. We're teaching them to understand the machine, to question whether it's working for them, and to change it when they need to. We're teaching them to be empowered, responsible, and ultimately happy citizens.

As long as we keep that purpose in mind, I would argue that there is little danger in asking corporations to help us achieve it where they can. Imagine how entertaining education could be if the advertising industry focused their budgets, technologies, and human resources on improving the educational 'user experience' for children.

Education cannot be a competition between companies.

Despite being deeply optimistic about the role of companies and corporations in education, I do have some reservations about *how* this might be implemented.

Chief among these is the concern that companies may become competitive in terms of their educational offerings. As we have mentioned already, the absence of a level playing field is a significant problem in our current economic model. Allowing our children's education to become yet another uneven battleground does not appeal to me, either as an entrepreneur or as a parent.

To ensure that we keep the competitive side of business away from our children's education, it would be important to create an environment where companies are heavily encouraged to collaborate on the educational content they create.

This collaboration serves two purposes. Firstly, it is able to protect our children from being in the middle of a battle between major corporations. Secondly, however, companies working together may present opportunities to show a 'joined up' approach to learning.

For understandable reasons, children are taught different subjects in isolation. This makes ideas easier to understand, and allows teachers to focus on the areas that they are particularly skilled in. It doesn't actually reflect the world we live in, however.

Great ideas require bringing together experts from across the academic spectrum, just as I have tried to do as I created this book. Encouraging collaboration between different companies may give children a real-world lesson in the power of collaboration and teamwork.

Not just wishful thinking

I'm aware that the idea of asking corporations to engage in refining, presenting, and broadcasting educational materials may seem deeply troubling to some readers, and somewhat fanciful to others.

Hopefully, the explanation I have offered of how I believe companies should be allowed to engage with our educational system, and the safeguards and concerns I have raised, may allow you to feel more comfortable with the idea that we can allow companies to play a role in educating our children.

There are risks in every decision we make, but I believe that the risks of allowing companies to contribute to the cognitive processing of educational content, with the caveats I have described, outweigh the risks of continuing with a deeply underfunded educational system and our existing advertising models. Importantly, the potential benefits of changing our educational system are profound.

These changes might seem radical, but they are absolutely possible. In the next chapter, we are going to look at some of the ways in which we can incentivize companies to act in ways that benefit all of society, including engaging more with education.

Chapter 10
Homo Ludens and 'AdEdTech'

"The time has come to realize that supersensible knowledge has now to arise from the materialistic grave."

- Rudolf Steiner

Chapter 10 Executive Summary:

- Replacing traditional ads with regulated educational content could present a win-win scenario for both advertisers and consumers.
- Using the power and know-how gained by the advertising industry over nearly a century, the advertising sector can help our children to learn more, better, and faster. Freeing up time for exploring their creative or artistic talents.

- Adding Advertising to Education Technology (AdEdTech) can facilitate desired elementary learning below conscious awareness, putting neuromarketing to the best possible use.
- By starting grassroot movements to promote AdEdTech, you have a unique opportunity to call upon advertisers and regulators to improve child mental wellbeing and restore educational imbalances as the antidote to a universal AI that risks becoming anything but human-centric.

Entering the solutions space

In this final chapter, I am going to put forward a couple of ideas for very specific policies that could have a dramatic impact on the amount and type of advertising children experience. The aim here is to move from a situation where advertising is arguably contributing to mental disease to one where it is actively beneficial to humanity.

It's important that the solutions we produce are sustainable, and don't create new or unexpected problems. The ideas presented in this chapter are based on the premise that disruptive innovation might help restore cultural imbalances causing mental disease.

I would like to stress that my ideas are merely intended as food for thought. There is no single step that will 'solve' the position we are currently in. I have tried to present ideas that are both innovative and achievable, but it's important that we don't let dogma prevent us from adapting or adjusting these as our media landscape changes.

Possible option: Ad-free periods

One serious option is to have set periods of time where advertising is simply not permitted. Ensuring that there are opportunities for children's brains to rest from the constant onslaught of advertising can have a dramatic impact on their wellbeing, and their brain development.

Obviously, this would pose major challenges, both logistically and socially. We're no longer in an era where banning television advertising during programming aimed at children would prevent them from seeing adverts. Much of the internet is funded by advertising, and removing this (especially if carried out by a single country unilaterally) would be both difficult and disruptive. But that doesn't mean we can't make a start.

Not all advertising is equally harmful. Video advertising typically attracts our attention (and disrupts child development) more than images, and text-based advertising is the least disruptive. It would be firmly within the realms of possibility to require streaming services to remove adverts during the times that we know their use by children peaks. Social media sites could also be required to deliver ad-free content to children during these time periods. And now that the packaging industry is starting to experiment with printed and wearable electronics using smart LEDs/OLEDs, even the traditional text-based labels might dynamically display branded content in compliance with new mental health guidelines.

I'm not suggesting that this will solve the problem, but it would represent a significant first step towards reducing our current marketing overdose. Not only would children have time away from adverts to recover and be exposed to fewer adverts overall. We would also be sending a powerful social message that we will not permit our children to pay the price or higher profits for corporations.

Possible option: Replace ads with educational content

This can help to set the stage for a further move towards protecting our children from the harmful effects of advertising. Once we, as a society, have fully acknowledged the potential harm of advertising aimed at children, we may be ready to make further requirements of major corporations.

Instead of spending on advertising to create their brand, companies could take responsibility for contributing to the development and broadcasting of carefully curated, peer-reviewed, high quality educational content.

This isn't about expecting the company that manufactures your fridge to teach your kids about WWII. We don't want corporations to create their own narrative or curate content themselves. Instead, this is about finding content that we all know children need to have at their fingertips, and using the power of advertising techniques (including neuromarketing) to make this material more enjoyable to process, understand, and memorize. Elementary learning on autopilot.

Limiting the ability to display advertisements will, of necessity, free up some portion of the advertising budget of major multinationals. With well-designed regulations, companies above a certain size could be heavily incentivized to devote some portion of that budget to contributing to the development, broadcasting, and user experience of educational content.

In practice, it's likely that (careful) regulation wouldn't be required to encourage companies to contribute to some form of educational content. If this was the only type of brand-building available for several hours of each day, people would see educational content as the opportunity it is.

I would argue that the place for regulation in corporate-provided education is in ensuring the educational content is of sufficient quality and scope. No one is suggesting that corporations should be able to 'teach' our children anything they consider educational with no oversight. That idea is enough to make my blood run cold.

Remember, we're looking for solutions that are well-considered, sustainable, and that don't come with loopholes or unexpected surprises. Careful regulation would be needed to ensure that companies were producing accurate, peer-reviewed information in an accessible and age-appropriate way. The advertising sector can contribute, in particular with the presentation and user experience of the educational content, in order to facilitate cognitive processing much in the same way brand associations are learned on autopilot.

Deploy the immense power of advertising, for education rather than direct profit

We've been talking throughout this book about the immense power that comes from neuromarketing tools. We've examined how they are able to measure people's emotional responses to the images or videos they are presented with. They can help advertisers and marketers understand what makes a message memorable and measure, how well we recall information. They can even highlight when something is confusing us.

Doesn't that sound an awful lot like the skills of an outstanding teacher?

These techniques and tools are incredibly powerful. As I've said before, if they weren't so powerful, we wouldn't be nearly as worried about how they're being used. Schools and education systems simply don't have the kind of funding that would be required to be able to actually use these techniques to help our children learn but major corporations do.

Using the power and knowledge accrued by the advertising industry over nearly a century can help our children to learn more, better, and faster, freeing up time for free, explorative, and natural play which is known to foster creativity.

Obviously, this kind of content doesn't in any way replace the need for great teachers who can open discussions, offer critique, and help children interact intelligently and respectfully with complex, nuanced ideas. But by taking on some of the 'information delivery' side of teaching, corporations can free up teachers' time and energy.

Helping our children to learn the information they need with tools designed for optimum results *and* easing the burden of overworked teachers sounds pretty good to me.

It's also worth noting that rote learning, whilst often valuable, isn't engaging or inspiring for children, and it can be a bit of a chore for adults as well. But this is an area where advertising and neuromarketing tools can excel. If rote learning happens 'behind the scenes' without any real effort on the part of children, they are able to retain their joy of learning and inquisitiveness about the world. And that's priceless.

Advertising-*inspired* educational content frees up time for your child's wellbeing

Our current approach to education requires that children spend long periods of time every day sitting (mostly) still and being (mostly) quiet. Obviously, this does become an important skill in adulthood, where most of us need to spend long periods of time every day sitting at a desk working when we'd much rather be doing almost anything else (even though we know that it's not great for our physical health).

Although they will need to learn this skill at some point (and concentrating through boredom is definitely a skill), it's counterproductive to try to force them into it too early.

In many parts of the world, the old-fashioned methods of teaching, with a teacher at the head of the class dictating to silent children, have already been cast aside because they're just not effective. They don't reflect how children learn.

Children learn by doing, by interacting with the world and with each other in unscripted settings. They learn about their world, but they also build up their own resilience, curiosity, and excitement. They're creating the building blocks of their own future wellbeing, as well as improving their wellbeing at the moment, simply by balancing their intellect with their creative, more intuitive minds. Think 'streetwise'.

We've already explained that advertising is able to use advanced techniques to provide a lot of information in a short space of time in a way that ensures it's remembered. This efficiency, if applied to educational content, will free up more of our children's time for exploration, play, and wellbeing.

Benefit: Levels the playing field for humanities

Governments have a huge number of plates to keep spinning at any one time, and a huge number of different priorities, many of which are in direct competition with each other. They have to make difficult decisions about where to spend *our* money.

One example of this is how governments (including local governments and school boards) choose to prioritize the money invested in education. Governments across the world have, quite understandably, tried to push more and more students into Science, Technology, Engineering, and Mathematics (STEM) subjects. At a governmental level, this makes sense. These are also the areas that lead to technological innovations and, ultimately, drive economic growth. They're also the areas in which most companies are reporting a skills shortage.

As you might imagine from this book so far, I'm a huge supporter of STEM subjects. I'm not suggesting that we should scale back our efforts in this area at all. I am concerned, however, that children aren't always getting sufficient access to the arts and humanities sides of the curriculum.

We all need a well-rounded and complete education. In this book, we're focusing on the technological aspects of the advertising industry (for example, social media algorithms) and the impact that this has on developing brains. We've also talked about the philosophy of consciousness, how we go about making social and political change, and how subtle differences in cultural expectations can lead to dramatically different corporate behaviors. This falls firmly on the humanities side of the coin.

A well-rounded education, encompassing the creative arts, is important for the very highest-quality innovation, but it's harder for governments to see the immediate advantages of, for example, having more linguists, poets, or artists. Nevertheless, social sciences subjects and the creative arts provide a huge amount of satisfaction, insight, and meaning to many people's lives. The most significant breakthroughs for human kind, like Einstein's relativity theory, are the result of exceptional interaction between well developed left *and* right brain hemispheres. Einstein viewed taking music breaks as an important part of his creative process. In addition to music, he was a proponent of 'combinatory play' — taking seemingly unrelated things outside the realms of science (art, ideas, music, thoughts), and blending them together to come up with new ideas.

This is where companies being more closely involved with education may be able to balance the scales a little. If their aim is to build positive associations with their brand, companies may well also be involved in helping students to understand music theory or art appreciation, as well as more analytical subjects.

Tax exemptions: The carrot rather than the stick

So far, we've mentioned regulation as an important factor in how we ensure that companies are acting in the best interests of society, as well as their shareholders. This isn't the only tool political leaders have available to them, however.

Despite some of the suggestions I've made so far, I have a strong preference for creating incentives to encourage companies to do the right thing, rather than using rules and regulations (and the associated bureaucracy) to constrain their decisions.

Unfortunately, we are currently in a position where we are having to undo a series of inadvertent incentives (such as increased attention to polarizing content). Now is the time to think carefully about the tools available to us, and how we can direct them to create social good, rather than sow divisions.

As we move towards a media environment that emphasizes the brain health and mental wellbeing of our children, our focus should shift progressively to providing significant tax incentives to encourage companies to collaborate on educational content to make it more accessible for children. Companies are doing a great job of driving innovation in advertising and marketing and finding exciting new tools to facilitate this. Tax incentives are a mechanism for maintaining that progress while directing their efforts toward outcomes that are ultimately beneficial to society as a whole, rather than harmful.

The next steps

From the very beginning of this book, I've said that this will have to be a shared mission. Clearly, changing the most familiar and uncontested interface of our present day economy, namely the Big Tech advertising industry, is not going to be a one man job.

If you're concerned by some of the problems in our current system that I've highlighted, there are a few things that you personally can do.

Amplify the conversation

Social media algorithms aren't the only way to amplify a signal. Talk about what you've learned with the people around you. Share your concerns with other parents. Tell people about this book, and discuss the ideas that resonated most with you. Even something as simple as writing a review of this book helps to raise our profile, helps our ripples reach more people and hopefully helps turn the tide.

Stay curious, inquisitive, and engaged

I've included a section at the end of this book with a few recommendations for reading that I think you'll find interesting and informative, but don't stop there. Read a variety of different opinions. Question both the status quo and the proposed solutions. Create your own journey of learning.

I'm not pretending that I have all the answers. I'm open to new ideas. If you find a potential solution that I haven't seen, I'd be delighted to hear about it. This is a team effort.

Talk to people in power

Political leaders are going to be key in creating the type of change I am advocating for. As we know, politicians respond to the issues their constituents are most concerned about. Ask them about their plans to tackle the problem of increasing mental disease. Ask them how they are supervising the content that is being recommended to our children by AI. Challenge their vision in terms of solutions.

Highlight the importance and urgency of this issue. Make your feelings heard. Make waves, not just ripples. Write to your political representatives. Ask questions.

Together, we can transform our current media ecosystem into something that serves us, our families, and our children.

Recommended reading

The Case Against Reality: Why Evolution Hid the Truth from Our Eyes by Donald Hoffman (Author) | August 13, 2019

Decoding Jung's Metaphysics: The Archetypal Semantics of an Experiential Universe by Bernardo Kastrup (Author) | March 1, 2021

Brief Peeks Beyond: Critical Essays on Metaphysics, Neuroscience, Free Will, Skepticism and Culture by Bernardo Kastrup | May 29, 2015

Entangled Minds: Extrasensory Experiences in a Quantum Reality by Dean Radin Ph.D. (Author) | April 25, 2006

My Big Toe: A Trilogy Unifying Philosophy, Physics, and Metaphysics: Awakening, Discovery, Inner Workings by Thomas Campbell | Dec 9, 2007

Inner Engineering: A Yogi's Guide to Joy by Sadhguru (Author) | September 20, 2016

Our Mathematical Universe: My Quest for the Ultimate Nature of Reality – Deckle Edge, by Max Tegmark (Author) | January 7, 2014

The Biology of Belief 10th Anniversary Edition: Unleashing the Power of Consciousness, Matter & Miracles by Bruce H. Lipton (Author) | October 11, 2016

Neurobranding: Strategies for shaping consumer behavior by Dr Peter Steidl (Author) | April 19, 2018

Noise: A Flaw in Human Judgment by Daniel Kahneman (Author), Olivier Sibony (Author), Cass R. Sunstein (Author) | May 18, 2021

Thinking, Fast and Slow by Daniel Kahneman (Author) | April 2, 2013

Science Delusion by Rupert Sheldrake (Author) | January 1, 2012

Consequences of Capitalism: Manufacturing Discontent and Resistance by Noam Chomsky (Author), Marv Waterstone (Author) | January 5, 2021

Capital and Ideology by Thomas Piketty (Author) | March 10, 2020

Sapiens: A Brief History of Humankind – Illustrated by Yuval Noah Harari (Author) | February 10, 2015

Humankind: A Hopeful History by Rutger Bregman (Author) | June 2, 2020

Reset: Over identiteit, gemeenschap en democratie Hardcover Dutch Edition by Mark Elchardus (Author) | October 14, 2021

Nudge: Improving Decisions About Health, Wealth, and Happiness Hardcover – Illustrated by Richard H. Thaler (Author), Cass R. Sunstein (Author) | April 8, 2008

What Kind of Creatures Are We? (Columbia Themes in Philosophy) Part of: Columbia Themes in Philosophy by Noam Chomsky | Jul 15, 2020

Modern Man in Search of a Soul by C. G. Jung (Author) | December 11, 2021

Knowledge in a Nutshell: Carl Jung: The complete guide to the great psychoanalyst, including the unconscious, archetypes and the self by Gary Bobroff (Author) | May 15, 2020

Contemporary Homo Ludens by Halina Mielicka-Pawowska (Author, Editor) | September 1, 2016

Education First!: From Martin Luther to Sustainable Development (STIAS) by Wolfgang Lutz (Author), Reiner Klingholz (Editor) | July 14, 2017

The Metaphoric Mind: A Celebration of Creative Consciousness by Bob Samples (Author) | September 1, 1976

Excellence Now: Extreme Humanism Hardcover by Tom Peters (Author) | March 30, 2021

Jung`s Red Book For Our Time: Searching for Soul under Postmodern Conditions by Murray Stein (Editor), Thomas Arzt (Editor) | October 11, 2017

Notes

Introduction - The who and the why

1. In his 1976 book "The Metaphoric Mind: A Celebration of Creative Consciousness" Dr. Bob Samples, actually didn't claim he was quoting Einstein; instead, Samples was presenting his personal, educated interpretation of Einstein's perspective. The phrasing evolved over time, and by 1997 someone had placed quotation marks around the descendant expression and had assigned the words to Albert Einstein, presuming they rightfully captured the essence of his perspective on the subject.

2. Doing the groundwork: philosophical and scientific underpinnings to solving big problems

1. https://www.essentiafoundation.org/analytic-idealism-course/

3. Trends in (consumer) neuroscience

1. Science, Technology, Engineering, and Mathematics (STEM)

6. Making capitalism work for us: How research bridges the gap between advertising and education

1. In his May 2021 publication 'Noise', Nobel prize winner, Daniel Kahneman explains how AI might be used to better meet those judicial needs.

7. Democratizing Consumer Neuroscience

1. ESG stands for Environmental, Social, and Governance. Investors are increasingly applying these non-financial factors as part of their analysis process to identify material risks and growth opportunities.

9. the ultimate teasers - Education on autopilot

1. STEM stands for **Science, Technology, Engineering, and Mathematics** in an educational context.

Printed by Amazon Italia Logistica S.r.l.
Torrazza Piemonte (TO), Italy

50196599R00131